THE TRINITY DIET

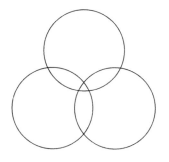

THE
TRINITY DIET

By **Stephen Steeves, CCN, CTN**

Contributions by **Amy Steeves and Jason Steeves**

LUCID BOOKS

AUTHOR'S NOTE

THE INFORMATION contained in the book reflects the author's experience and is not intended to replace the advice of your own personal physician. It is not the intent of the author to diagnose or treat disease. The intent is only to assist you in gaining and maintaining a healthy lifestyle.

In the event that you utilize this information of your own free will to achieve your own personal health goals, the publisher and the author assume no responsibility.

DEDICATION

I AM truly grateful for my wife, partner and best friend Amy who has been by my side through sickness in searching for answers to my sufferings. Amy's diligence in helping make the work at the Nutrition and Health Center a success must certainly be noted. I feel she is truly praiseworthy for her attention to all the details in helping write this book.

We are deeply grateful to our contributing editors Kelly Hall, Shauna Wallace, Carol Kelly and Angela Peiris for sharing our vision and skillfully helping us bring this book to fruition. They spent many hours diligently pouring through this book with detailed precision and always with a cheerful happy heart. We love you dearly!

CONTENTS

MY PERSONAL
MIRACLE

"And they have conquered him by the blood of the Lamb and by the word of their testimony, for they loved not their lives even unto death."
REVELATION. 12:11 (ESV)

IN 1982, I married my sweetheart, Amy Brusnahan. We were looking forward to an exciting life together, full of possibilities. Amy and I were very active, spending much of our time together running or working outside. We were not married long before we were blessed with Amy's first pregnancy. About five months later, I started experiencing unusual and severe back pain. Over the next few weeks, it rapidly progressed into a shooting pain that traveled from my lower back down through my legs. I could barely walk without pain, but because my job required the lifting and pulling of large cables, I reluctantly agreed to go see an orthopedic surgeon.

I remember the day Amy and I received the devastating diagnosis—ankylosing spondylitis, a severe and incurable form of rheumatoid arthritis that was only going to get worse. I was given drug therapy for pain management, and because there was no cure for the condition, I was told to expect to be confined to a wheelchair by the age of forty or fifty (not exactly the mid-life set of wheels I had envisioned). I pictured having to watch my children run and play while I sat constrained on the sidelines; perhaps I would have to walk with a cane, a walker, or be pushed in a wheelchair by Amy.

I imagined a life in which I couldn't be active in the way I was accustomed to—as a man, a husband, and father. As we walked out of the doctor's office into the parking lot, a small voice from within me said, "There is another way. Seek out another way." These words of life and hope inspired my first steps toward a new beginning. I began to seek knowledge about health and healing, refusing to just believe and accept what I was told. I was not about to receive the negative diagnosis that had been given me.

So how does a man destined for a wheelchair turn a disease-cursed life into an amazing life full of health? "Working out your salvation" is a phrase Paul uses in the New Testament. The word *salvation*, or *"sozo"* in the Greek, means salvation, healing and deliverance. This is a process we work out in life. You do not just wake up one day and find yourself in the state of abundant health. God sets a path before you, but you must take it. It does not come easy—hence the word, 'work'.

So, I began my work, and when it came to studying about the human body, I was insatiable. The more I learned, the more I wanted to know. I wanted to understand everything about how our bodies work. A short time after beginning my study in clinical nutrition, I also began to study the Bible. To my amazement, it was full of truths concerning health and healing. Now I had two passions to follow: studying nutrition and studying scripture. I discovered that physical health is intimately connected to spiritual and mental health. When one suffers, the others suffer as well. The "trinity" of human design is unique. God created us in His likeness –intricately connecting us to Himself and His creation.

The more I studied about the body, the more I realized how miraculously we are created. I could not deny the existence of a Grand Designer. The Bible says we are "fearfully and wonderfully made" (Ps. 139:14), designed in God's very image (Gen. 1:26). I found that my journey quickly extended beyond simple management of the superficial disease that was present in my body (believe me, arthritis is no joking matter). Instead, what lay before me was a great work of understanding and purpose that would lead not only to the healing of my body, but also to the salvation of my soul.

Jesus Christ is the vital component that has made all of my work a success. As my relationship with Jesus grew, the Creator God revealed the path He had for me to work out my salvation—one step at a time. I found great assurance in Philippians 1:6 when Paul says, "*...being confident of this, that He who began a good work in you will carry it on to completion until the* *day of Christ Jesus."* In the Old Testament, King David himself spoke these words of life: *"It was good for me to be afflicted so that I might learn your decrees"* (Ps. 119:71). I pray these words will also bring comfort to others who are afflicted.

Some say fate is unchangeable and destiny is set. However, this has not been my experience. In the face of every obstacle, there is a choice to be made. I chose then and continue to believe now that God has destroyed the darkness that descended with my diagnosis. I ventured out on a new path, to a life of health, activity, and vitality. If I had allowed myself to be defined and defeated by this curse, ignoring the freedom that Jesus Christ bought for me, there is no doubt in my mind that today I would be in a wheelchair, bound in pain and disoriented from prescribed medications that were meant to control my symptoms and discomfort.

I know in my heart that God allowed me to go through the pain of a debilitating illness so my story would align with His greater story of healing. In this way He would be glorified through me, which is His plan for all of us. This book includes a number of testimonies, both of mine and of others, who have experienced God's healing through nutrition. My greatest desire is that God would enable me to share the inspiration and knowledge He has given me with others, who will then be motivated to strive toward abundant health—the ultimate purpose of this being, that God will be glorified. I want to see people truly believe that the sacrifice of Jesus continually works to heal all things and draws us closer to God.

The last twenty-five years of my life have been a first-hand, living research study on the abilities of the body. As a result, I am a very different person today. Recently, I celebrated my 50th birthday and am experiencing the best health I have ever had. I can go for a jog with my wife, play basketball with my son, or squat with one-hundred and fifty pounds on my back. I am not crippled; I am healed and continue to remain healed.

Applying the principles of *The Trinity Diet* and lifestyle has enabled my body to heal from a crippling arthritis. These truths have also allowed Amy and me to raise three children to adulthood without the use of antibiotics, medicines or any medical intervention. Had we faced a serious trauma or accident, we would have sought medical attention. However, for the last twenty-five years, whenever our family has been sick, we have applied the principles of *The Trinity Diet* successfully and allowed our bodies to heal themselves.

We know this is the will of God the Father—not just for our family, but also for everyone. Jesus spent His ministry saving, healing and delivering the people of God. My work is to fuel people with truth and knowledge about how their bodies function and to give them hope for a future—free from sickness and pain. I pray that the wisdom I have gained and shared with family and friends for more than a quarter century will enable people to take control of their own health. Do not let fear lead you down a path of destruction and possibly death. As Paul says in 2 Timothy 1:7, *"For God has not given us a spirit of fear, but of power and of love and of a sound mind."*

Before you heed this or any other human advice, I encourage you to pray. Paul suggests that we pray, and pray about everything. Seek out wisdom. The Bible says that if you ask for wisdom, God will give it to you. God has a plan for your life and He will fulfill it as you follow His commands in all things. It is my prayer that you will know freedom from sickness and disease. As you strive to live for God and balance your body, soul and spirit by following the principles of *The Trinity Diet*, may you be more fully equipped to fulfill the calling that God has placed on your life. If you would like more information please visit our website: www.NutritionandHealthCenter.com.

THE NEW **NORMAL**

"The thief does not come except to steal, and to kill, and to destroy.
I have come that they may have life, and that they may have it
more abundantly."
JOHN 10:10 (NKJV)

E VER NOTICE how conversations these days either revolve around
or wind up on the topic of physical ailments? "Aunt Agnes has yet
another collection of kidney stones... Grandmother is suffering stroke
after stroke... Father has congenital heart disease...!" Or what about the
conversations that start with or contain statements like, "I'll be happy
when...I lose twenty pounds...I can walk through the store without getting
out of breath, etc...?" It seems as if feeling abnormal is the "new normal."
There are so many people wandering in and out of doctors' offices in
search of what is wrong with them. It seems as though we are trying to
label our ailments in an attempt to blame something for making us feel so
bad all the time. Are we as a rule, so lost and desperate to be found, that
we will take on any label—even a negative or debilitating one? Is being
labeled by the name of a disease what you really desire, or do you want to
find your way to true abundant life and health?

There are thousands of people in doctors' offices receiving devastating
news right now. It happens every day. It happened to me when I was
diagnosed with arthritis. It was like a curse spoken over me, but I refused
to accept it. Deuteronomy 30:19-20, tells us about curses:

> "I call heaven and earth as witnesses today against you, that I *have set
> before you life and death, blessing and cursing; therefore choose life, that both you
> and your descendants may live; that you may love the LORD your God, that you*

may obey His voice, and that you may cling to Him, for He is your life and the length of your days; and that you may dwell in the land which the LORD swore to your fathers, to Abraham, Isaac, and Jacob, to give them."

Words are influential. We have a choice of which words we will receive and which we won't, as well as those we will speak over others and ourselves. Consider how differently it feels to be called a "winner" rather than a "loser." The sacrifice of Jesus is about restoration, hope, and healing for the body, soul and spirit. Jesus redeemed us from the curse and we are living under an open heaven enabling us to hear and receive God's healing.

The state of health in America is declining, and not because of pestilence, famine, bacteria, infected waters, or poverty. It is because we do not honor God's creation—our bodies. We are mindlessly eating and thereby disconnecting from the source of our food, the Lord, the provider and sustainer of life. Quite honestly, my greatest fear is that God's people won't be able to share the hope of Jesus because we are distracted and disoriented from ingesting all the refined, processed, hydrogenated foods that we were never designed to eat in the first place.

God handed Moses a set of dietary and cleansing laws for the Jews, demonstrating the level of importance He places upon the way we feed and care for our bodies. I find it most interesting that Jesus' approach to life was centered on worship. Each and every act of the day was one of health, healing and a right relationship with the Father. Many accounts of Jesus' teachings were shared over a meal. The Bible tells us that Jesus ministered at weddings, upper class dinner parties, mountainside picnics, and at an intimate supper with His closest friends. He even prepared for his disciples a grilled fish breakfast on the beach. Through Christ's example, we learn that preparing, serving and eating meals, can and should be acts of worship.

Sad as it may seem, most Christians cannot tell you the last time they ate mindfully, much less worshipfully. So, if the majority of Americans are led by their bellies, it is not difficult to understand how obesity and diabetic statistics are off the charts in America. Unless we are mindful and purposeful about everything we put into our bodies, while choosing to stay continually in God's presence, we run the risk of becoming a negative statistic—just another health casualty. Paul gives us instruction in his letter to Ephesus about becoming a people "whose end is destruction, whose god is their bellies, whose glory is in their shame" (Phil. 3:19). We would be wise to heed his warning.

Weight management can be challenging, but you can achieve and maintain your ideal body weight through balance. In 1962, research statistics of the Center for Disease Control (CDC) showed that the percentage of obesity in America's population was 13 percent. By 1980, it had risen to 15 percent, and by 1994 it was up to 23 percent. By the year 2000, the obesity progression in America had reached an unprecedented 31 percent!

In the sixteen years we've had our Nutrition and Health Center, we have watched the annual cost of obesity in the United States rise. This directly correlates to the number of clients we see, who struggle with weight problems. Obesity has led to an increase in the number of people suffering from type 2 diabetes. In fact, as a nation, we are losing the fight against diabetes. There has been an approximate 30 percent increase of cases in the past ten years. Obesity is also associated with an increased risk of heart disease, hypertension, various cancers, adult onset diabetes and reduced life expectancy, to mention a few. The annual cost of treating conditions associated with obesity is draining Americans financially as well.

Dieting isn't helping, either. Like a pendulum, swinging from one extreme to the other, fad diets often promise unrealistic weight loss goals. Some of these diets claim that you can lose up to ten pounds a week! The problem is however, just like the pendulum, the weight will swing back to the other extreme as well.

Fortunately there is hope! Through a properly executed *Trinity Diet* program, a male will burn an average of eleven calories per pound of body weight and a female ten calories per pound of body weight each day. The maximum amount of fat loss possible in a week is between four and six pounds. Although fad diets may produce a greater initial weight loss, 90 percent of people regain that weight and often times more. This happens because the eating program does not address the underlying causes of weight gain. In order to reach and maintain your ideal weight, it is imperative that you identify the causes of weight gain and make fundamental lifestyle changes.

The foundation of *The Trinity Diet* is not a question of "What?" but "Who?" In whom will we be found? Amy and I arrived at the conclusion that the "Who" and foundation of our lives is Jesus Christ. If we can manage to remember that we no longer live for ourselves, but for Jesus Christ, we will operate out of healthy spirits that in turn lead us to make healthy choices. This is an essential understanding we must have especially when caring for ourselves and our families. From this prayerful position, we can see how a relationship with the Lord affects even our physical bodies, and helps return us to a more focused way of living.

The Human Cell

We are the most unique of all creation in that our bodies are made up of trillions of individual cells working together. There exists a trinity of macronutrients (proteins, carbohydrates and fats—discussed later) that has a strong hormonal effect on cells. Each cell has a specific function and uses nutrients to exercise energy at the cellular level, whether in our heart, lungs, intestines or leg muscles. This trinity of macronutrients has different effects on cellular health and hormone function. It also regulates body systems to function at an optimal level so that everything from what we eat, to the amount we eat, is brought into balance.

Hormone Balance

Weight-loss diets are usually not biochemically sound because they focus on short-term results, not lifestyle changes for long-term benefits. This typically produces what is known as "yo-yo" dieting. Nutritionally deficient diets create muscle tissue loss and produce a lower metabolic rate because muscle, the furnace which burns the body's fuel, is lost. This is why after going off of a diet, weight is rapidly regained as fat. Successive diets make the problem worse!

Simply counting calories or lessening fat intake may reduce weight; however, weight loss for most becomes a loss of lean muscle mass and not fat loss. Correct dietary balance can prevent this from happening. In fact, with the proper balance of menu planning and exercise, we have seen personal gains in lean tissue (muscle, bone, organs and blood). This knowledge is easily gained through Bio Impedance Analysis (BIA) testing, which measures body composition.

Proteins, fats and carbohydrates (the trinity of macronutrients) have many benefits in addition to providing calories. The balance achieved between these different foods can have a significant, positive impact on your body's hormone production, improving the way they signal every cell in your body. These hormones are the key to unlocking a more efficient metabolism for proper weight management. An unbalanced ratio of the trinity of macronutrients can negatively influence the levels of three powerful hormone regulators: insulin, glucagon and serotonin. Imbalance occurs when food intake consists of too many refined carbohydrates—sugar, white flour etc., poor quality fats, and not enough protein. This can cause instability in body fat, which many naturopathic physicians consider the leading cause of disease

Disease Process and Regeneration

Many times, people seek synthetic hormones for weight loss. This is not the answer. Taking these hormones, either for pancreas (insulin) or thyroid (thyroid hormones), cause these glands to slow down and stop their production. This is called atrophy, which occurs as the gland begins to weaken due to the lack of use. Like muscles that become weak without exercise, these hormone producing glands will deteriorate over time with disuse. However, I have come to know that the Lord has designed all body cells to regenerate. Therefore, feeding and nourishing the gland or organ can provide the foundational materials necessary for reconstruction. Certain foods and herbs have properties that help rebuild tissue cells in the body. Milk thistle, for example, has known properties that restore the integrity of the liver and protect liver cells from damage. In fact, studies have shown that milk thistle increases liver-produced proteins as much as 40 percent.

Each day our bodies go through a breakdown process; every day and night, the body repairs and regenerates if adequate nutrition support is available. When the body is not getting the adequate rest and repair it needs, and toxicity and distress levels are in excess, the body begins to break down and the disease process begins. Thankfully, this progression can be reversed with better lifestyle choices. We have seen hundreds of individuals with diabetes, hypoglycemia, high blood pressure, elevated cholesterol, triglyceride excess and weight problems find metabolic stability and better hormone balance with the application of *The Trinity Diet*.

Tenisha entered our office as an insulin dependent diabetic. After two months on *The Trinity Diet* program, she was able to go off her insulin pump and maintain stable blood glucose naturally. She still struggles, as we all do, with balancing *The Trinity Diet* components and her life of stress, but she strives to make better lifestyle choices. She seeks more constructive food options and is becoming more renewed each day. She chose to make a difference in her own health because so many people depended on her.

"Everything is permissible—but not everything is beneficial. Everything is permissible—but not everything is constructive. Nobody should seek his own good, but the good of others." (1 Corinthians 10:23)

We must stop long enough to consider if our behavior is constructive for the kingdom of God, and if what we are doing as active agents for the Lord is beneficial to our bodies, our families and our communities that depend on us. Eating mindfully and worshipfully is a discipline worth striving for. It is our prayer that you will join us in upending the current normal and move into God's ideal life for you, a life of vibrancy.

THE TRINITY **DIET**

"Now may the God of peace himself sanctify you completely,
and may your whole spirit and soul and body be kept
blameless at the coming of our Lord Jesus Christ."
I THESSALONIANS 5:23 (ESV)

WHEN I speak to groups about nutrition, I love to ask the question: "Aren't you glad you are here and not in one of the best hospitals in the city?" Of course, there is a resounding "Yes!" or "Amen!" from everyone in the room. No one wants to end up in a hospital, and yet so many of the lifestyle choices we make everyday will cause the majority of us to be there one day.

What is the one thing all adults want more than riches, fame and success? In reality, health is truly the greatest of all earthly blessings. Nothing can be fully enjoyed without health, and most things can never be attained without it. The way my family and I have found abundant life and blessings is by following a lifestyle and discipline called *The* Trinity *Diet*—a life balance of body, soul (mind, will and emotions) and spirit.

The Trinity

To understand *The Trinity Diet*, we must first define *trinity*. The concept of the trinity is unique to Christianity and represents the idea that God exists as three persons—the *triune* God. Tri means three and unity means one. This gives us the word *trinity* meaning three in one. It is a way of acknowledging what the Bible reveals to us about God:

- God the Father is fully, completely God.
- God the Son (Jesus) is fully, completely God.
- God the Holy Spirit is fully, completely God.

Yet there is only one God.

Even in nature there are many mysteries of the trinity that are clearly evident. Water, for example can exist as a liquid, a gas (steam), or a solid (ice). In each case it remains fully and completely water (H_2O), although uniquely distinct in form. In our limited minds, we do not have the capacity to fully understand the Triune God. However, from the beginning, we see the way God reveals Himself in scripture. Notice the plural pronouns *us* and *our* in Genesis 1:26:

> "Then God said, 'Let *us* make man in *our* image, in *our* likeness, and let them rule over the fish of the sea and the birds of the air, over the livestock, over all the earth, and over all the creatures that move along the ground'" (emphasis mine).

Humans are formed as triune beings, completely whole—created with bodies, souls and spirits. Because of this fact, with divine authority, we are able to draw from our physical wisdom, spiritual wisdom, and the wisdom of our minds to make balanced choices. A good mental image of this would be to visualize a triangular based pyramid with the elevated point representing God. In this illustration, all three points of the base, work together under God's guidance and discipline. Without the headship of God, this would become a two dimensional, fat figure—a triangle. Each point would struggle for dominance as there would be no defined head. After more than twenty-five years of research, I have come to realize that the framework of *The Trinity Diet* has allowed me to heal completely. The name *Trinity Diet* originated as a way to help people understand the importance of proteins, carbohydrates and fats and their connection to the spiritual. Whatever affects the physical body, then affects the soul (mind, will and emotions) and the spiritual. Think about waking up in the morning. What's the first thing you typically have to do? Most people use the restroom before thinking about anything else. We take care of our bodies before we can do anything else.

The Trinity Balance

In fifteen years of clinical nutrition work with clients who for the most part consume a standard American diet, I have come to realize that the most difficult aspect of educating people lies in the area of how to feed their bodies. As a clinical nutritionist, naturopath and phytotherapist, one of the first concepts I teach my clients is the importance of balancing the macronutrients. Macronutrients (protein, carbohydrates and healthy fats) are essential foods without which we would be unable to sustain good health. In contrast to micronutrients which are consumed in smaller quantities—such as vitamins, minerals, enzymes, or phytonutrients—macronutrients are the largest of all nutrients that humans consume. For example, the average female needs approximately sixty grams of protein per day, but only an average of two to ten grams of vitamin C.

Our bodies are temples of the Holy Spirit, precious gifts from our Father in Heaven. Macronutrients are essential for our bodies to function consistently and prevent degeneration and disease. Therefore, we must feed our bodies a balance of what I call the trinity of macronutrients (protein, carbohydrates and fats) in order to achieve optimal health. Just as God is perfect in three persons, so our diet is ideal when our dinner plates are balanced.

Unfortunately, fad diets full of misinformation have left a majority of Americans completely baffled when it comes to making good meal choices. Many diets have cut out or drastically reduced one of the trinity of vital macronutrients. Other diets may require excessive ingestion of a particular macronutrient leading to an imbalance in biochemistry that could ultimately lead to disease or even death. An imbalance of these macronutrients may not catch up with you right away, but in time, your body systems will degenerate giving disease a foothold. Understanding *The Trinity Diet* balance will help take away the confusion about what and how much to eat.

The premise of *The Trinity Diet* is to show how the trinity of macronutrients can mirror the concept of the Triune God. In this context, protein would symbolize God the Father, carbohydrates—Jesus the bread of life, and oil/fat of life—the Holy Spirit.

In the following chapters, I will coach you on how to create a worshipful experience with God through the appreciation and disciplined balance of all that you eat. I will share information on why we get sick, how to cleanse and how to practically apply this eating program to your life. Also included is a variety of fabulous family recipes that we have used for years and information on how to correctly and effectively exercise your body.

It is our prayer that you will always look to God to meet your needs in every area of your life. We pray this book will support you in seeking Him and will invigorate your life experience.

CHAPTER 3

PROTEIN:
THE FATHER GOD

"Yet for us there is but one God, the Father, for whom
all things came, and for whom we live."
I CORINTHIANS 8:6

PROTEINS ARE the foundational structures upon which all living cells
are assembled. The word *protein* comes from the Greek word *proteos*
meaning "of first importance or primary importance." As the Father God
is the head of the Holy Trinity, we therefore have placed protein at the
head of *The Trinity Diet*.

Protein is defined as any group of organic macromolecules that contain
carbon, hydrogen, oxygen, nitrogen, and usually sulfur. It is composed of
one or more chains of amino acids. Protein is a fundamental component of
all living cells and exists in all living things. All cellular structures require
protein for the proper function of body systems and it is essential in the
diet of all mammals for the growth and repair of tissue. The structure of
the eyes, skin, hair, nails and organs are all comprised of protein. Most
proteins exist in unique three-dimensional structures, which exemplify
and glorify the triune nature of God. This should not be a surprise given
the fact that God is the creator of all things (1 Corinthians 8:6).

The Cross of Christ: A Connective Tissue Protein

At the very foundation of the human cellular structure, researchers
have found a cross-shaped protein called laminin. This molecule, found
in the basement membrane, is a connective tissue protein used to hold

15

the entire body together. The structure of laminin serves as an amazing representation of the cross on which Jesus died to pay the penalty for the sins of all mankind.

Why did Jesus have to die? When Adam and Eve sinned in the Garden of Eden, humankind became eternally separated from God. A chasm of sin was formed that could not be overcome. Jesus' death on the cross however, provided a bridge of relationship back to the Father. Without the cross, we would remain completely separated from God. Jesus clearly explained this point. He tells us in John 14:16, *"I am the way and the truth and the life. No one comes to the Father except through me."* Jesus is the only way! Because of His vicarious sacrifice, those who confess Jesus as Lord and believe in their hearts that God raised Him from the dead, can now be reconnected back to the Father for eternity.

My friends, I pray you will see that Jesus is the one who holds everything together—even our bodies. Colossians 1:17 (NIV) tells us, *"He is before all things, and in him all things hold together."* Confrming this, John 1:2-4 says, *"He was with God in the beginning. Through him all things were made; without him nothing was made that has been made. In him was life, and that life was the light of men."*

Just as laminin connects everything in our bodies together, Jesus Christ is the "connection" we have to God the Father. Therefore, laminin can be seen as a representation of our eternal relationship and connection to the Father God through the work done on the cross by Jesus Christ.

Protein First

Since *protein* means "first," wisdom would suggest that when we consume food, we must be careful to include adequate protein because it is the most important macronutrient. As a family, when we plan our meals, we first consider what our protein serving will be. Chicken, fish, beef, lamb, turkey and game hen are the most common protein sources we choose. Occasionally, if we do not wish to eat meat at a meal, we select legumes such as black beans, pinto beans or lentils instead. Black beans are one of the highest yielding protein-rich beans available. Quinoa, a high protein grain, is also another great choice.

Dietary Laws

When choosing animal proteins for consumption, we always consider the dietary laws the Lord gave us in Leviticus 11 and Deuteronomy 14. "Unclean" animals are loaded with higher levels of toxins and are used as scavengers on the earth for cleaning up debris and dead material. The Bible identifes the raven, vulture, pig, owl, and hawk, as well as scavenger fish such as shrimp, lobster and catfsh as unclean. Many of these biblically unclean animals also possess high levels of cholesterol. By contrast, examples of "clean" animals include the cow, deer, buffalo, chicken, turkey, salmon, trout and bass. "Clean" animals have more efficient elimination systems, which make their meat purer for humans to consume and easier for our bodies to assimilate. (More information on toxins is presented in *Chapter 7: Cleansing and Detoxification.*)

In 1953, Dr. David I. Macht of Johns Hopkins University, conducted toxicity tests on "clean" and "unclean" animals based on the dietary laws of Leviticus 11 and Deuteronomy 14.[1] Dr. Macht concluded that the toxicity of the "unclean" animals was higher than that of the "clean" animals and that the correlation with the description in Leviticus was one-hundred percent accurate. Dr. Macht used a toxicology test, cited in peer-reviewed literature that was particularly good for zoological toxins and therefore relevant for testing kosher and non-kosher meat, fish, and poultry.

---

[1] Macht, D. (1953, September/October). An Experimental Pharmacological Appreciation of Leviticus XI and Deuteronomy XIV. *Bulletin of the History of Medicine, Vol. XXVII(Num. 5), 444-450.*

Vegetarians and Protein

In the beginning, God gave Adam and Eve *"...every seed-bearing plant on the face of the whole earth and every tree that has fruit with seed in it. They will be yours for food"* (Gen. 1:29). Scripture also says we are formed from the dust of the earth. Interestingly, protein is rich in nitrogen, which once was abundantly present in the earth's soil. Researchers have speculated, however, that the earth changed as a result of the great flood during Noah's life. Prior to the flood, meat was not consumed in the diet. The soil in the earth was rich in nitrogen which would have provided a higher yield of protein in the vegetation, providing the nutrients necessary for a vegetarian diet. After the flood, the soil was depleted in nutrients and thus the Lord permitted the addition of meat to Noah and his family's diet when He said, *"Every moving thing that lives shall be food for you. I have given you all things, even as the green herbs"* (Gen. 9:3 NKJV).

It seems most probable that the Lord allowed meat in our diet to help provide a balance of nutrition for humans due to the nitrogen- depleted soil. Here again, in the Old Testament we see the reference to "all things," referring to all living things, but specifically to animals that were meant for man to consume.

Often, vegetarians struggle with many deficiencies such as in amino acids, CoQ10, and B12. In my twenty-five years of research, I have discovered it is nearly impossible and certainly most difficult for humans to achieve dietary balance in their body chemistries when attempting to eliminate all meat.

Addison, who has been a client for many years, started living an exclusively vegetarian lifestyle. In six months time, Addison was full of yeast (Candida), her skin and eyes were yellow, and she had lost muscle tissue. She had the appearance of a malnourished person from a third world country. After quality meat protein was reintroduced into her diet for one month, the yellow in her eyes cleared and her skin returned to a healthy pink tone. She also regained the weight she had lost.

Although Addison's testimony is compelling, one should still note that vegetarians can obtain a balance of protein in their diet with supplementation of the correct nutrients. Foods such as legumes, beans, lentils, nuts and seeds have significant levels of protein. With careful evaluation of their personal caloric need, some can indeed live a vegetarian lifestyle.

The Missing Link

When assessing our clients at the Nutrition and Health Center, we have found that most are critically low in protein. It is rare to find an individual who does not have some form of protein deficiency. Either they aren't consuming enough quality protein or they simply are not absorbing it through the digestive process. The process of digestion begins in the mouth and is a critical part in the uptake of protein. The many stages of digestion are required to break the protein down into useable molecules called amino acids.

In our health clinic we perform a Bio Impedance Analysis test (BIA). This test enables us to determine an individual's lean body mass, which is supported and maintained by protein. It also indicates whether the person is gaining or losing lean tissues in their muscles, blood, bones and organs. By looking at the fat free mass (FFM), the basal metabolic rate (BMR—the number of calories burned per day), and activity levels, we can determine a client's specific protein needs. The FFM is everything within your body that is not fat. This includes muscles, organs, bones, ligaments and water. The FFM, or metabolically active tissue, is critical because it is where fat and sugars are burned as fuel.

Susan battled with her weight for years and finally went in for gastric bypass surgery. She lost some weight initially, but further testing revealed that she had also lost significant levels of lean tissue. Her body fat showed her to be obese at more than 40 percent fat. Susan came to my office complaining of digestive problems, fatigue, brain fog and anxiety. She felt worse than before her gastric bypass surgery. Susan is now balancing her health with *The Trinity Diet* program. She is losing fat, gaining lean body mass—including muscle tissue, and feeling much better. This is evidence that the body will begin to heal itself if proper nutrients are supplied. The healing power of God is in each of us. The Lord has heard Susan's prayers.

We are told in Matthew 7:7, *"Keep on asking, and you will be given what you ask for. Keep on looking, and you will find. Keep on knocking, and the door will be opened."* The word of God does not return void and your persistence in seeking Him and learning to walk in health will not be in vain.

Sarcopenia: Muscle Wasting

Sarcopenia, or muscle wasting, occurs in epidemic proportions today in the United States. As we age, proper protein intake is essential for the prevention of sarcopenia. The previously mentioned BIA test has become popular for measuring body composition, providing values for muscle, fat, intra-cellular water (ICW), extra-cellular water (ECW), basal metabolic rate (BMR) and phase angle which reflects cellular energy function.

The BIA test is done with an imperceptible electric current that passes through the body's tissues. The resistance created within the tissue provides readings that are used to calculate the body composition parameters listed below.

- *Phase angle* determines the integrity of the cell membrane–critical for hormone signaling. It also reveals the overall energy, health and function of the cell which is used to identify a person's biological age on the cellular level.
- *Fat free mass (FFM)* measures a person's overall fat-free mass and is an indicator of body composition factors such as muscle, bone, water, blood and connective tissue.
- *Fat percent and fat pounds* evaluate pounds and percentage of fat within the body. The fat compartment of the body is known to be a toxic dumpsite for materials that unhealthy bodies have difficulty removing.
- *Intra cellular water (ICW)* is a measurement of water contained within the cells of the body. This compartment becomes depleted in dehydrated individuals and those who do not have healthy cell structure. When the working components within the cell are deficient of various nutrients, the ICW compartment is diminished.
- *Extra cellular water (ECW)* is a measurement of water contained in the extracellular fluid space. An elevated ECW reveals toxicity in the body and can be addressed with a detoxification program to assist the liver, gallbladder, kidneys and lymph. *The Trinity Diet* also aids in the reduction of ECW.
- *Basal metabolic rate (BMR)* is an indicator of the calories the body burns in twenty-four hours at rest. As the FFM or lean mass increases, the calories burned increases. This is a critical factor to prevent muscle wasting which helps resist the aging process. Protein consumption

is critical for the maintenance of muscle tissue and proper calorie burning or BMR.

The Trinity Diet is crucial to the maintenance and balance of the BIA markers. The BIA is easy to perform and provides printable test results quickly. We perform this test on every client at our Nutrition and Health Center. Alternatively, you can find a local practitioner that performs BIA testing in your area.

An example of one of our client's BIA results, starting with her first consultation and following for several months, is included in this section. Marla is a fifty-six-year-old female client who began *The Trinity Diet* weighing in at one-hundred and seventy pounds. She was leading a very sedentary yet stressful lifestyle. Even without exercise, by implementing *The Trinity Diet* she was able to lose a total weight of thirty-two pounds—thirty of which was from fat alone. Generally, without exercise, a person will lose significant amounts of muscle, but Marla was able to balance her nutrition with supplements to achieve a healthier life, better muscle tone, and a stronger body. Here are her BIA results from September 5, 2006 to March 5, 2007.

DATE	5-Sep-06	16-Oct-06	22-Nov-06	3-Jan-07	5-Mar-07
HEIGHT	65.00	65.00	65.00	65.00	65.00
WEIGHT	170.00	155.00	151.00	149.50	138.00
AGE	55	55	56	56	56
RESISTANCE	519.0	558.0	511.0	505.0	511.0
REACTANCE	45.0	48.0	40.0	39.0	39.0
IDEAL/DESIRED WT	130	130	130	130	130
ACTUAL BMI	28.29	25.79	25.13	24.88	22.96
% ACTUAL FAT	39.7	36.6	32.7	31.7	27.1
LBS. ACTUAL FAT	67.5	56.8	49.3	47.4	37.4
FFM	102.5	98.2	101.7	102.1	100.6
ACTUAL BMR	1322	1285	1282	1282	1271

Marla's experience is typical of our clients who embrace *The Trinity Diet*. On this program, even without exercise, some people like Marla, can still maintain their lean tissue. With slight modifications in lifestyle, most people enjoy noticeable results both in body composition and in energy and quality of life.

The Calcium-Protein Matrix and Bone Health

Just as muscle is a matrix of protein, bone structure has a protein base as well. The proteins in our bones provide the structure to which minerals such as calcium can bind. The protein support structure in bone looks somewhat like the metal rebar placed in concrete to reinforce it and prevent cracks and breaks. Without adequate protein to hold the minerals in the bone, the bone structure becomes brittle and can break easily just like concrete would without rebar.

In the United States and Norway, we ingest large amounts of dairy products, consuming more than all the nations in the world. Yet, our diets are the highest in poor-quality calcium. These two countries have ranked highest in osteoporosis disease worldwide for many years. I would like to warn you, if you feel secure that your bones are strong because you drink milk, you are experiencing a false security. Milk products lack the proper form of calcium to be adequately absorbed into the body. Poor absorption leads to an excess of calcium that can deposit in the kidneys, arteries, and the gallbladder causing serious negative effects. This could be the leading reason why there are more than five- hundred thousand gallbladder surgeries performed in the United States every year. In addition, many of the proteins found in milk also cannot be absorbed correctly. This causes auto immune reactions in which the body attacks its own pancreas and the production of insulin becomes depleted, leading to diabetes. We have seen many insulin-dependent individuals with diabetes give up dairy products to see their insulin and glucose levels return to normal. Removing dairy, the antagonist, releases the burden on the immune system and allows the pancreas to return to its normal function. If you would like more details and research on the effects of milk on the human body, please visit *www. notmilk.com*.

Various tests can be performed to evaluate the balance of calcium and protein in a person's body chemistry. It is the presence of protein and the balance of the trinity of macronutrients and other bio-chemicals found in food that determines the overall health of the body. Healthy forms of calcium such as citrate, ascorbate, coral and microcrystalline are best for human use. Inorganic forms such as carbonate and oxide are not easily absorbed. They can deposit in organs and joints and cause gallbladder conditions, arthritis, and heart disease.

Neurotransmitters

Neurotransmitters are chemicals used to communicate, magnify and transfer signals between a neuron, or nerve cell, and other cells. All neurotransmitters for the nervous system are formed from amino acids—single units of protein molecules each with a specific function in the body. Many amino acid imbalances are due to environmental toxins, stress, genetics, and deficiency from poor food choices in the diet. Currently, tests that use urine and saliva are available to accurately measure specific neurotransmitters. A blood spot amino acid test can be ordered and performed in the privacy of your own home. With just a prick of the finger required, these test results will identify the missing chemicals needed for the production of neurotransmitters. Indicators for twenty amino acids in your body can then be evaluated to create a personalized supplement formula. These nutrients can correct many neurological disorders, fatigue, depression, anxiety and many imbalances. Because neurotransmitter balance is critical for optimal nervous system function, it should be assessed for ideal health.

Protein Essentials

Supplementing proteins and/or amino acids will provide the support your body needs each day to complete the repair process. *The Trinity Diet* helps ensure adequate intake of quality protein.

Humans require at least eight essential amino acids in their diet. These essential amino acids are the building blocks for the manufacturing of some fourteen other acids in the body, necessary for many critical functions involving brain neurotransmitters and enzymes which help you digest your food. A deficiency of protein amino acids can lead to fatigue, chronic pain, obesity, athletic over-training and poor athletic performance.

Muscle energy comes from the trinity of what are called the branch chain amino acids (BCAAs) – leucine, isoleucine and valine. These three essential amino acids make up approximately one-third of skeletal muscle in the human body. They are so powerful that they are used in the treatment of burn victims and energy disorders. Interestingly, these acids are most highly concentrated in muscle meat—another reason I believe the Lord allowed consumption of meat after the food. It seems His purpose for this was to help maintain energy function in the muscles.

Protein and Optimal Thyroid Health

Chicken, beef and other meats have an amino acid called phenylalanine, which the body breaks down to tyrosine, for the manufacturing of thyroxine (T_4). This is the major and most active thyroid hormone in the body. Without the proper amount of protein, the necessary building blocks for the production of T_4 are diminished, resulting in an under-active thyroid. Some of the other most common causes of an under-active thyroid condition include a high-stress lifestyle, poor digestion, and/or nutritional deficiencies of supportive nutrients such as iodine, zinc, selenium, B12, and B6.

Many individuals have relied on standard labs to evaluate their thyroid function. However, reference ranges for the blood values provided by these labs are extremely broad and are often used to label disease. Testing the blood, saliva and body temperature offers a more effective means for determining optimal thyroid function. I recommend a simple test discovered by Dr. Broda Barnes to evaluate thyroid function. Before getting out of bed in the morning, place a thermometer under your armpit and leave it there for ten minutes. Record the temperature and repeat for ten days. Any consistent values below 97.8 degrees indicate a sluggish and under-active thyroid function and suggest a need for further nutritional evaluation and support.

The use of thyroid support to increase metabolism and BMR is important for those who have a slow metabolism or sluggish thyroid. Most professionals today have limited knowledge when addressing issues on thyroid health. Typically, they only look at the thyroid stimulating hormone (TSH) to evaluate thyroid status. The problem with that is TSH is not a thyroid hormone. It is a pituitary hormone with a typical reference range of .4 to 5.5, which is a variation of 1,275 percent. This means a person with a value of .4 is considered normal, and a person with a value of 5.5 is acceptable as well. Given this wide range, how would you know where you should be?

The thyroid hormones that should be assessed, along with TSH, include triiodothyronine (T3), thyroxin (T4), and free T4, also known as T7. These are the actual thyroid hormones produced by the thyroid gland. Knowledge of these values provides for higher accuracy when assessing thyroid health. Optimal levels are quite different than the normal lab values and they represent the narrow path we should travel to achieve and maintain optimal health.

Like the gallbladder, the thyroid has become a popular gland for aggressive (not to mention invasive) surgeons to harvest. Thyroid diseases such as thyroiditis, goiter or hashimoto's are usually treated with radioactivity or surgery, followed by a lifetime prescription of thyroid hormone. There is a better way! Thyroid health can be restored with adequate nutritional support using nutrients like organic iodine, protein, tyrosine, B6, zinc, B12, folic acid, and the trinity of macronutrients to balance the energy needs of the whole body.

We have helped many hopeless individuals regain optimal thyroid health. For example, Dorothy came into my office on a synthetic thyroid hormone. Her doctor told her, "Your thyroid is dead, and you must stay on this medication for the rest of your life." Within three months of being off synthetic medication and on restorative nutrients, she lost thirty-five pounds and went back to her doctor for testing. The doctor spoke these words: "It's a miracle. Now, instead of a dead thyroid yours is very active."

One of the main thyroid aggravators is gluten. In our clinic, we have seen growths on the thyroid begin to disappear when gluten is removed from the diet. Gluten is found in many grain products and many processed foods as an additive. This protein, found in grains such as wheat, is known to cause autoimmune reactions within the body. When gluten is removed from the diet, the thyroid is able to function normally again. Once more, we see the testimony of the healing power that is in each one of us. We are created by God to restore, regenerate and heal—even a once dead thyroid gland.

Hormone Health and Protein

Hormones have become the hot topic of the twenty-first century. All hormones in the body are derived from protein; therefore, adequate protein is necessary for optimal hormone balance and function. Hundreds of women and men with hormone imbalances find better health and fewer annoying symptoms when applying *The Trinity Diet*. Unfortunately, the mainstream medical approach to address the symptoms associated with hormone imbalance is to prescribe a bio- identical hormone. The problem with this method is that the delicate hormone balance of the body is easily disrupted. When we consume a bio-identical hormone, the gland in the body that is supposed to produce that hormone shuts down its own natural production. Endocrine glands such as the thyroid, adrenals, and pituitary will then atrophy or waste away due to lack of use.

Every gland requires adequate nutrition to produce a hormone. God designed the body to produce adequate hormones from what He has provided in nature. If you suspect that you might be suffering from a hormonal imbalance, specific information on how to support hormones and body systems using natural herbal remedies is given in *Chapter Seven*. You may also need to seek professional help from a local naturopath or clinical nutritionist who can safely guide you back to health.

Cancer and Protein Loss

Cancer is an epidemic today. An alarming one out of every two people contracts the disease in their lifetime. Living in the Houston area, with the highest rate of cancer and the largest cancer clinic in the world, many people who have been diagnosed with cancer seek out our clinic for help. I have found that the common denominator in most of my clients with cancer is a very serious protein deficiency. Sarcopenia is a common factor when they are evaluated through body composition analysis, and blood proteins such as albumin and globulin are usually always low as well, also signaling the lack of adequate protein.

Critical Testing: Protein and Amino Acid Levels

Diets rich in quality protein sources provide adequate amino acids which we now know are the building blocks for almost every tissue in the body. When we don't eat quality proteins or our bodies aren't able to digest them, it can lead to chronic conditions. Medications, chronic or increased stress, poor eating habits and aging (including poor eating habits due to aging), also contribute to this lack of protein. Unfortunately, even when a person consumes an adequate amount of protein, it does not guarantee an optimal supply of amino acids. Poor eating habits, hurried eating, and weak digestive function can cause malabsorption of proteins. Accordingly environmental toxins and stress tend to overburden the liver and interfere with its ability to break down protein into the amino acid units necessary for optimal health. These protein building blocks are critical for the prevention and treatment of many chronic illnesses. To ensure an individual has adequate intake and absorption of these proteins; I recommend various functional assessments to determine an individual's biochemical protein needs.

Your Protein Needs

In order to properly calculate your daily protein needs, follow these three simple steps.

1. Determine your lean body mass or fat free mass using a BIA test that is easily acquired and performed by a health professional or trainer.
2. Determine your activity factor as a multiplier by selecting one of the values listed below:

   _____ .5 (sedentary individual)

   _____ .6 (light fitness training such as walking)

   _____ .7 (moderate training, around three times weekly)

   _____ .8 (daily aerobics or moderate weight training)

   _____ .9 (heavy weight training at least five days per week for one hour)

   _____ 1.0 (heavy sports training and weight training five or more days per week for two or more hours per day)

3. Use the following formula to calculate your specific daily need for protein in grams (a minimum per day is sixty grams):

   Lean body mass X activity factor = daily protein requirements in grams

   _____ X _____ = _____

Throughout the years, this particular calculation has proven to be the easiest and most accurate way to assess personal individual protein needs. Once you determine the grams of protein your body requires each day, you can take the next step of finding quality protein to eat while making sure your body is able to properly digest that protein.

You will find that dividing the grams into five meals per day and eating every three hours will help you achieve your daily protein goal and give you sustained energy. Protein is necessary to balance glucose, which is stored as energy after a meal. Protein also helps the body maintain hormonal balance, burn fat as fuel, and lower inflammation associated with disease conditions.

Quality Protein Choices: Fifteen to Twenty Grams Per Serving

Each of the following quality proteins offers fifteen to twenty grams per serving and should be considered for your daily requirements.

Eggs	3 whole/5 egg whites
Chicken or game hen (free-range)	3 ounces
Fish, salmon, trout, bass	4 ounces
Tuna (water-packed	3 ounces
Turkey (free-range)	3 ounces
Beef (hormone- and chemical-free)	3 ounces
Beans, lentils, tofu	8 ounces
Yogurt (low-fat, low-lactose)	1 1/2 cup
Cottage cheese (low-fat, soy preferred)	1 cup

A three- to four-ounce serving of meat is approximately equal to the size of a deck of cards when cooked. We do not recommend dairy products because of the lactose and casein proteins that can interfere with immune function and disrupt healthy digestion. Lactose is a milk sugar that can suppress the immune system, and casein cannot be broken down and absorbed by humans. Therefore, avoiding both is advisable.

Medical foods can also be an excellent source of quality protein. These products are medically formulated to be rich in quality and easy to digest. There are a number of great medically formulated foods on the market. In our clinic, we carry Metagenics and each of their Ultra Meal, Ultra Clear, and Ultra GlycemX products have fifteen grams of protein per serving. Designed by Metagenics to treat metabolic syndrome, these products also offer far-reaching benefits for blood sugar balance, hormone balance, weight management, high blood pressure and cholesterol balance. In addition, Ultra Clear assists in the complete detoxification of the liver, cleansing it of systemic poisons that accumulate daily in our toxic world.

With more than twenty years of experience in the nutrition field, I do want to caution you to pay very careful attention to the quality assurance procedures reputable professional supplement companies are using today. The quality of food supplements can vary a great deal, and the old saying, "You get what you pay for," holds especially true in this industry. When evaluating a company and its products, you will want to research thoroughly. Some factors to analyze when attempting to make an informed decision concerning supplement choice include:

- raw ingredients used
- heavy metal testing
- extraction methods
- sources of raw material
- pesticide residues
- identifcation testing of herbs.

At the Nutrition and Health Center, our top three supplement companies are Standard Process, Metagenics, and Perque. Together, they have more than one-hundred and forty years of experience and only sell to health care professionals. Once you have selected a quality product, I am confident you will never regret your decision to supplement *The Trinity Diet* with quality proteins for best absorption. Confrmation of your good decision is sure to follow in the form of improved health.

CHAPTER 4

CARBOHYDRATE:
JESUS, THE BREAD OF LIFE

"I am the bread of life. Your fathers ate the manna in the wilderness, and are dead. This is the bread, which comes down from heaven that one may eat of it and not die. I am the living bread, which came down from heaven. If anyone eats of this bread, he will live forever; and the bread that I shall give is my flesh, which I shall give for the life of the world."
JOHN 6:48-51

A S ANOTHER member of the Triune God, Jesus—the bread of life, is represented by carbohydrates in *The Trinity Diet*. Jesus plays a vital role in our lives as Christians, as do carbohydrates in our health. In the beginning, Jesus was present with the Father, speaking all life into existence (see John 1). Through faith in Him and by grace alone, our bodies, souls and spirits have been saved from eternal separation from God. We have been given life! Thanks be to God! In like manner, without carbohydrates, our bodies would not have the necessary energy, or life, to function properly. Carbohydrates are the proprietary source of energy for all body functions. While proteins and fats can be converted into energy, this does not occur until carbohydrates are depleted. This process requires more cellular energy than burning carbohydrates, so carbohydrates are the body's preferred source for energy and are needed for optimal functioning.

Eighty percent of energy used in the cell is derived through the burning of carbohydrates for fuel. Carbohydrates are reduced to glucose for use in human cells for energy and remain the only source of energy for the brain and red blood cells. Therefore, when people do not consume quality carbohydrates, we start to find conditions such as attention deficit disorder (ADD), headaches, bi-polar disorders and attention deficit hyperactivity disorder (ADHD). Even dementia and Alzheimer's are linked to improper blood sugar utilization in the brain.

Individuals who have blood sugar lows are not eating enough quality carbohydrates to store sugar in the muscle and the liver for later use. The result is a rapid drop in blood sugar, sometimes within minutes after eating a high carbohydrate meal. These blood sugar lows affect our minds, wills and emotions, causing a lack of focus and giving the devil an opportunity to cause mental confusion. Consuming a diet that includes *unrefined* carbohydrates, proteins, and fats, enables us to store and maintain blood sugar for healthy brain function.

Ann came to our office with emotional and physical ailments which she had suffered from for many years. She used food as an emotional tool to help her deal with stress and the struggles of her life. Ann could not imagine living a day without crackers and chips. However, when we prayed together, she immediately knew the Lord would give her the strength to live this new life and she committed to depend on Him and not food. In the following months on *The Trinity Diet*, she lost nearly fifty pounds and acquired a greater energy, joy and zeal for living.

One morning she received a phone call from her child's school and the voice on the other end said, "Your daughter is having a seizure." This was not the first time this had happened, and in the past, her response to the situation was one of sheer panic. In fear, she would race to the school, speeding and running traffic lights. However, this time she calmly got into her car and drove to the school. Full of peace in her mind, body, and spirit, she prayed to the Lord as she went. Later, when telling the story, she was amazed at how calmly she responded to this very stressful situation. She attributed her ability to remain sound, to the lifestyle changes she was making as she followed *The Trinity Diet*.

Blood Sugar Balance and Frequent Eating

As you can see, blood sugar can significantly affect your quality of life. Understanding where your blood sugar levels should be and knowing how to rectify any imbalances will help you maintain energy and focus throughout the day. If you take your blood sugar (glucose) level before eating in the morning, the ideal reading should fall between 75 and 90. Typical medical reference ranges for glucose are between 60 and 100, but this is a wider than optimal range. In order to determine how well you are metabolizing glucose from a meal, purchase a glucose tester from almost any supermarket and test your glucose two hours after you eat. This is called a two-hour post-prandial reading. The ideal range for glucose two hours after a meal is between 75 and 90.

It is especially important to watch your quality carbohydrates when following any diet. I cannot tell you how many people have come into my office feeling miserable because they are following a yeast-free diet that completely excludes carbohydrates, such as fruit and bread. As soon as they can eat fruit and bread again in moderation, a smile comes on their face and they seem hopeful that they can enjoy life once again. When we limit carbohydrates to such an extent, it is difficult to go about our daily activities. If our main source of fuel comes from carbohydrates and we cut it from our diets, we operate less effectively.

How often we eat is as important as what we eat. After a healthy, balanced *Trinity Diet* meal that includes protein, carbohydrates, and fat, the body has the ability to store glucose in the liver and in muscle for approximately three hours. At that point, the average person has burned his or her stored glucose. Blood sugar drops and the hunger process begins again. At this critical time, another *Trinity Diet* concept comes into play, the trinity of time. Ideally, we should eat every three hours, whether we feel hungry or not. This enables the body to store energy and keep a balance that will maintain energy for every cell all day long. This concept will also prevent stress response in the body, allowing it to lose weight and come to optimal balance. My personal eating times are six o'clock and nine o'clock in the morning, noon, and four o'clock and seven o'clock in the evening.

Like other mammals created similar to humans, consuming food frequently is important. Most mammals eat continuously throughout the day. I imagine that's how it was for Adam and Eve when they lived in the Garden of Eden, an environment perfect for optimal health. They had food at hand that was not processed, had no preservatives, no synthetic hormones, no toxic residues and no pesticides. Can you imagine strolling through a lush, vibrant garden with your spouse, free of all stress, plucking fruit, leaves and nuts from massive bushes as you walk? Then perhaps you would head off toward a pristine river to swim, drying afterwards in the sun and reclining in the shade while eating tomatoes, cucumbers and basil!

We may not live in that perfect utopia any longer, but the same principles that led to a nine-hundred- year life span for Adam, hold true for us today.

Life Is in the Blood

Leviticus 17:14 says that blood is the life of the flesh. It is the blood of Jesus, shed on the cross which gives life to the body, soul, and spirit. Similarly, the blood in our bodies carries glucose throughout the body as the primary fuel for all cells. Remember, glucose is the most reduced form of a carbohydrate and is critical for balanced energy in the body. In our clinic, we have observed a distinct connection between disease and low energy, which is often due to an imbalance of *The Trinity Diet* nutrients. Jesus is the divine healer, and similarly, unadulterated carbohydrates provide the necessary energy for the body to repair itself. All disease involves issues with energy production in some way or another, which is why, following a balanced *Trinity Diet,* can help provide restoration for most any health condition.

Carbohydrate Disease: An American Epidemic

Unfortunately, poor quality carbohydrates are available in abundance and are ignorantly consumed in mass quantities daily. These refined carbohydrates are found in most packaged foods on store shelves and include breads, pasta, cereals, crackers, chips, etc. These forms of carbohydrates have a high glycemic index (GI), which is a measure of the rate at which a particular carbohydrate influences blood glucose levels. They tend to cause blood sugar to rise dramatically, followed by a plummet, making you to feel tired and many times depressed.

Several years ago, the common belief among researchers was that fat was the cause of many diseases. Consequently, everything in the commercial market became a low- or no-fat product. Once the fat was removed, the only thing left of the trinity of macronutrients was poor quality carbohydrates and poor quality protein. Since simple refined carbohydrates are so inexpensive to manufacture and can be kept preserved for long periods of time, they have become the commercially profitable choice of ingredients in food distributed on grocery store shelves. The saying, "Some is better than none" does not hold true in this instance. These simple refined carbohydrates are really a false food designed to deceive consumers into believing they are getting the real thing.

In Mark 13:5-8, Jesus said to them:

Watch out that no one deceives you. Many will come in my name, claiming, 'I am he,' and will deceive many. When you hear of wars and rumors of wars, do not be alarmed. Such things must happen, but the end is still to come. Nation will rise against nation, and kingdom against kingdom. There will be earthquakes in various places, and famines. These are the beginning of birth pains.

In this scripture, Jesus tells His disciples what will happen before He returns for His faithful followers. There will be those who claim that they are Jesus, but in fact, are liars attempting to deceive. Building on our comparison, we can identify untold numbers of products on the market that also claim to be the "real thing." Like those who impersonate Jesus, these items are also deceitful! The processes of refining, enriching, fortifying, bleaching, etc. have stripped these carbohydrates, and they cannot live up to the energy and sustainability of the original. They are "false" carbohydrates.

False carbohydrates, which I call adulterated carbohydrates, **are not real food** for the body and are a critical factor in the cause of many of the degenerative diseases today. The nutritious elements are removed from food to prevent spoiling while it is shipped and stored in warehouses. The living enzymes that help to digest the food are removed along with many other nutrients that would otherwise give the carbohydrate life potential for the body. The products then sit on the shelf indefinitely, with no life in them, serving mostly to increase the profits of the manufacturer. This is all done with your dollars and at the expense of your health.

These unstable, partial carbohydrates are full of sugar and artificial ingredients that draw us away from the healthy carbohydrates we were intended to consume and even commanded to consume in Genesis 1:29. This is certainly the plan of the enemy to pervert the perfection of food originally formed by the hand of God for the Garden of Eden. God's food was designed to be life for our body, which is now the temple of God. First Corinthians 3:16-17 challenges us, *"Do you not know that you are the temple of God and [that] the Spirit of God dwells in you? If anyone defies the temple of God, God will destroy him. For the temple of God is holy, which [temple] you are."*

I believe the issues of food and lifestyle are the biggest reasons Christians are toxic and sick today. When people partake of the system of this world by eating packaged, refined, enriched, fortified, bleached, processed food without the knowledge of their detrimental effects, they have been deceived. Commercials and magazine ads deceivingly portray new low-calorie snacks or amazing new sweeteners as wonderful healthy products. Ignorantly and without question, we purchase these items. We have become a boxed-in, over-worked, hyperactive, sterilized people—some army of God! We must break free of the deception Satan has used to bring bondage on God's people through the misuse of food, in order to be the power-packed, victorious, enduring army of strong warriors that He desires!

Taking in quality complex carbohydrates will provide a more abundant physical life full of energy and strength. We need a proper balance of carbohydrates in our diets. One of the most frequent questions I hear is, "With so much information out there, how do I know what I should eat?" My response is, "Eat foods that rot, spoil and decay, but be sure to eat them before they do."

Jesus said, *"...you shall know the truth and the truth shall set you free"* (John 8:32). Ask for wisdom, and He will give it to you and lead you into all truth. His word is the source of strength we need to withstand the temptation of everything that does not build up our bodies, souls and spirits in Christ Jesus.

Fat Loss Made Easy

Not only is it imperative to eat the right carbohydrates, but we must also eat the right amounts. When we consume too many carbohydrates, the result is stored body fat. Excess intake of carbohydrates prevents the body from burning fat as fuel and elevates insulin production. This turns the carbohydrates into fat, which is then stored in the body. Over consumption of carbohydrates also elevates triglycerides, which contributes to heart disease, high blood pressure and stroke.

A balanced carbohydrate intake, as encouraged in *The Trinity Diet*, actually promotes fat loss. In order to determine the quality of a carbohydrate, you can look at its GI. Carbohydrates that break down quickly in digestion and release glucose rapidly into the bloodstream are considered high GI. Examples of these include refined carbohydrates and certain fruits and vegetables. Hybridized produce, which is higher in sugar content, also falls into this category. Carbohydrates that absorb slowly into the bloodstream have a low GI. The benefit of low-GI foods is remarkable and powerful in gaining whole body health.

For best health results, select carbohydrates that have a low GI, while limiting yourself to no more than two servings of high-GI carbohydrates per day. Remember, each mealtime should be no more than four hours apart, and three hours is preferred. Each meal should be a balance of protein, fat and carbohydrate. Medical foods (discussed in the previous chapter) are great for snacks because they provide quality protein, carbohydrates and fats in one single serving with added vitamins and minerals to balance blood sugar for optimal energy function.

When selecting carbohydrates for a meal or snack, it is important to understand portion sizes. The serving sizes below are equivalent to thirty grams or approximately 50 percent of your plate when eating a meal. A small person weighing less than one-hundred and fifty pounds would do well on a thirty-gram serving at each meal. Remember, you will be eating every three hours and don't need to over eat at any one meal. Larger individuals weighing more than one-hundred and fifty pounds and those who are active may need even more grams at each meal. A calculation to determine your daily calorie needs is provided in chapter three.

As you can see in the chart of serving sizes below, a thirty-gram serving of a low-GI food is more food than a thirty-gram serving of a high-GI food—so you get more bang for your buck.

Fruits (high GI)	1 cup
Fruits (low GI)	2 to 3 cups
Vegetables (high GI)	1 cup
Vegetables (low GI)	2 to 3 cups

Thirty-Gram Servings of Carbohydrates

The following information can be used to help you achieve a proper balance of low- and high-GI carbohydrates in your daily *Trinity Diet*.

High-GI Grains, Pastas and Cereals

(These should be limited to a maximum of one serving per day.)

Cereals (whole grain)	1 ½ cups
Pastas	1 ½ cups
Sprouted grain bread	1 ½ slice

Low-GI Vegetables

Asparagus	Bean sprouts	Beets	Beet greens
Broccoli	Brussel Sprouts	Cabbage	Cauliflower
Celery	Chard	Chives	Cucumber
Collard	Eggplant	Endive	Greens
Kale	Leeks	Lettuce Okra	Onion
Parsley	Pimento	Pumpkin	Radish
Red Pepper	Spinach	String bean	Turnip
Watercress			

High-GI Vegetables

Artichoke	Carrots	Corn	Green peas
Lima beans	Parsnip	Potato, sweet	Potato, white
Squash	Yam		

Low-GI Fruits

Apple	Apricot	Blackberries	Cantaloupe
Cranberry	Grapefruit	Guava	Kiwi
Lemon	Lime	Melons	Orange
Papaya	Peach	Plum	Raspberries
Strawberries	Tangerine	Tomato	Watermelon

High-GI Fruits

Banana	Blueberries	Cherries	Dates
Dried Fruits	Figs	Grapes	Kumquats
Mango	Mulberries	Pear	Pineapple
Pomegranate	Prunes	Raisins	

Scriptural Bread

Bread can be an excellent source of quality carbohydrates, if made with the proper ingredients. Jesus is the bread of life, and the Lord has given us a recipe for bread that can be a source of life to our cells. I consider this bread to be the healthiest of all breads and the recipe is found in Ezekiel: "*Also take for yourself wheat, barley, beans, lentils, millet, and spelt; put them into one vessel, and make bread of them for yourself*" (Ezek. 4:9). This bread is full of many plant sources such as sprouted beans and lentils, which provide carbohydrates, as well as fiber and protein to make it a balanced carbohydrate source. Sprouted grains and beans yield a higher quality of nutrients, and the additional source of protein from the beans helps to stabilize blood sugar and allows for better storage of sugar in muscle cells for later use. Jesus served food to thousands, and in each case, He chose a complete trinity diet of food when using the protein and fats in the fish and carbohydrates in the bread.

Sadly, bread in the United States and many other countries has been severely adulterated. Most of the seeds are now hybridized to maximize profit, and these hybrid seed crops are not what the Creator meant for our body. As a result, we suffer from disease because we fail to farm and grow food the way God intended. The Lord clearly instructed in Exodus 23:10, "*You shall sow your land for six years and gather in its yield, but {on} the seventh year you shall let it rest and lie fallow...*" When the land can rest for a year, the soil is replenished with nutrients for a better and more nutritious crop. Since this is no longer a common practice in most mass-producing food industries, you can either make your own bread, or you can purchase sprouted- grain breads that are found in the freezer section of your local health food store or supermarket.

Sugar: Cancer's Favorite Food

A great number of diseases, including cancer, are the result of excess intake of refined carbohydrates. From observing individuals in our clinic, we have found that excessive refined carbohydrates in the diet, cause a breakdown in health and an occurrence of most disease conditions. When we consume excessive amounts of refined carbohydrates, it creates a vicious cycle in which the body wants more and more. Because it is absent of any substantial nutrition, the body is never satisfied. Even in the hours close to death, a cancer patient will crave sugar, which continues to poison the body and weaken immune function. This gives the cancer fuel to increase activity.

The great news is that reducing the glycemic load in food choices actually helps strengthen the body to fight cancer. Cancer cell activity is increased by excess sugar in the diet. In fact, the tests that are performed to view cancer cells use sugar to cause these cells to be more active, and therefore more easily seen. Consequently, those who have diets high in refined sugar will be at higher risk of cultivating cancer. If you want to strengthen your body's ability to avoid and fight cancer, it is critical to reduce your consumption of refined carbohydrates. That means avoiding foods that contain white flour, white sugar or high-fructose corn syrup.

In his book, *Beating Cancer with Nutrition*, Patrick Quillen presents an in-depth look at how sugar feeds cancer. He says, "Cancer cells feed almost exclusively on sugar." This is why we must do our very best to eliminate refined sugar from our diets, yet the opposite is happening. According to Quillen, "The average American consumes 20 percent of calories from refined white sugar, which is more of a drug than food." He also explains, "Elevating blood glucose in a cancer patient is like throwing gasoline on a smoldering fire." I recommend Quillen's book for anyone who wants to know more about the many issues associated with cancer.

Body Pain and Inflammation

Jesus Christ is our deliverer who leads us not into temptation but delivers us from evil. The evil one will lead you (as long as you are willing) into that which steals, kills and destroys your health thereby preventing you from walking in abundant life on this earth. Physical pain is a favorite tactic Satan will use to distract us from our created purpose to serve and worship the Lord. People who are suffering with pain may find it extremely difficult to notice the presence of God daily. It can be extremely challenging to fulfill the calling on our lives when we are in pain. Many pain syndromes, from fibromyalgia to arthritis, can be improved by following the simple principals for health and healing that God has given us. This is what we are sharing here in *The Trinity Diet*.

While working with clients in our clinic, we have found that refined carbohydrates increase inflammation in the muscles and the brain. I am convinced that God never intended carbohydrates to be a problem and in their natural state, they rarely are. Jesus bore our iniquities and sufferings so that we would not have to suffer if we listen to Him and follow His ways. I do not believe we will escape life without pain, but we need not inflict pain on ourselves by consuming refined carbohydrates that increase inflammation. We need to remember that we are free to choose good health.

If you are suffering from pain in your body, one of the first things you can do is to stop eating sugar. When you shop, read all labels and do not purchase any of the products that have sugar listed in the ingredients on the label. Read carefully, as sugar is many times disguised as sucrose, dextrose, and high-fructose corn syrup.

Attention Deficit and Depression

Carbohydrates possess an important support for mental clarity and thinking. The brain, which weighs only three pounds—a small fraction of our body weight—consumes one-fifth of the body's need for carbohydrates (glucose) as fuel to function. In fact, the brain uses glucose as its only source of energy. Therefore, I believe most mental problems such as depression, attention deficit, forgetfulness, brain fog and fatigue are primarily caused by depleted blood sugar from lack of quality carbohydrates or hypoglycemia.

A two-year-old boy named Memphis was brought into our office with his mom one day. From the moment he arrived, he was extremely cranky and whining. I asked the mother for permission to check his blood sugar (or glucose) and found it was 52, which is very low (an optimal level is 75 to

90). She quickly gave him some carbohydrate food, and he soon stopped whining and became happy. The mother did not, however, choose to give him a quality carbohydrate. Soon the happiness of the child faded and Momma was looking to soothe him once more with refined carbohydrates. This reaction, known as hypoglycemia, is common in American youth today. This is one of the reasons why the rate of diabetes and attention problems in children is at an all-time high and continues to rise.

Mothers that feed their children only a bowl of cereal, toast or refined sugars in the morning, without a balance of protein, carbohydrates and fat, will soon find their children suffering from countless health issues. Most parents today are not teaching healthy eating habits to their children. I believe it is our responsibility to model and teach healthy lifestyle habits to our families. Amy and I are seriously perplexed when we eat out at a restaurant and see parents eating a salad and some vegetables with their meals, while they give their child pasta, macaroni, spaghetti, cheese, bread and sweets. Just the other day, we saw a parent at a restaurant hand their child a bagged, refined, junk-food meal they had picked up at a drive-through window, while they ordered a more healthy selection for themselves.

Some researchers believe that today's high-tech, fast-paced, fast- food generation must change these dangerous lifestyle and dietary habits, or they will not outlive their parents. At breakfast and at every meal, we all need a balance of protein, carbohydrates and fats in order to enjoy an alert mind, steady emotions, optimal health, sustained energy, and so much more. A typical breakfast in our home is a smoothie of frozen fruit, such as cherries or strawberries, with protein powder and fax oil added. This provides a perfect balance of the Father (protein), Son (carbohydrate) and Holy Spirit (fats)—*The Trinity Diet* of macronutrients. Another balanced breakfast might include whole grain toast with an apple spread as a source of carbohydrate, some local yard eggs and/or some natural turkey sausage cooked in olive oil. You will be satisfied and energized for many hours.

One of the greatest threats to our children's health presents itself at school every day. Temptation is conveniently provided by our public and other school systems through vending machines full of junk food. These are available in abundance, and the mighty dollar is the main reason for the disregard of the health of our children. When our son, Jason, went to public school in the sixth grade, he decided to take advantage of his freedom from mom and dad and indulge in sweets from the vending machines. (How could our precious boy do this kind of thing?) Jason's behavior became like that of the many ADHD kids that get mislabeled every day. We even received a call from the school asking us to take him to get tested for the disorder. We knew at this point that we needed to sit Jason down to discuss the problem. We firmly made it clear that if he continued to use lunch money for sugar foods and drinks at school, there would be consequences. We then set up a better breakfast program that included a more balanced consumption of trinity foods, and we sent additional food with him to keep his brain well fed. We never heard back from the school again after taking the responsibility to properly nourish our son. According to a Fox News Report, the nation's largest beverage distributors have agreed to stop nearly all soda sales to public schools after reports of rising childhood obesity rates caused a wave of regulations through school districts and legislatures.

There is absolutely no doubt in my mind that refined carbohydrates and sugars are the number one cause of ADD and other related mental disorders; however, these conditions are not exclusive to children. When these children with ADD and depression become adults, the same problems exist, but they are often covered up with medication and stimulants such as coffee, sodas and aggressive sport drinks. Many people have returned to my office after following *The Trinity Diet* and have reported that depression was no longer an issue. When blood sugar is low, the brain does not have the adequate fuel to function and mental focus is lost. A *Trinity Diet* will provide the balance necessary to provide fuel to the brain continuously and to reduce symptoms associated with ADD and depression.

Genesis chapter twenty-five presents an interesting story of how low blood sugar might have played a part in bringing about some serious consequences—Esau sells his birthright to his brother Jacob, for a bowl of stew. After working in the field all day, Esau, the first-born, returned home very tired and hungry. He certainly was not able to grab a quick meal "to go" as we can today. Esau was a desperate man, obviously experiencing low blood sugar after working hard as the scripture says he was weary. Jacob was looking for an opportunity to gain God's favor with the birthright blessing that belonged to Esau, so he decided to use food to bribe Esau for his birthright. Esau was weak, and his mind was most likely foggy due to a lack of glucose in his blood to feed his brain. He was unable to make a wise decision and sold his birthright for a bowl of stew! How many times a day do we try to make decisions when we have low blood sugar? At times, these wrong decisions could change our whole future like it did for Esau.

Carbohydrates Bring Peace

Unadulterated carbohydrates release an anti-stress hormone called serotonin in the brain. This hormone is an ambassador of peace and well-being to the body. John 14:27 says, *"Peace I leave with you; my peace I give to you. Not as the world gives do I give to you. Let not your hearts be troubled, neither let them be afraid."*

The Lord brings peace to our spirits, souls, and bodies and it is amazing that carbohydrates similarly, in their natural state, bring a peaceful feeling of satisfaction. The key is to only consume unadulterated carbohydrates. Refined carbohydrates can cause excess serotonin, making you very relaxed and sleepy after meals. Not only that, they could cause an addictive eating pattern. Many who have emotional and spiritual insecurities and struggle with anxiety, use refined carbohydrates as a way to cope and detach from reality. This creates a vicious cycle that can lead to hopelessness, obesity and disease. As in all things, the Lord gave us His perfect way to peace and health. We only have to choose it.

Carbohydrate Sensitivity Test

The following survey is designed to evaluate a person's sensitivity to carbohydrates and their resistance to insulin and hormones in the working cells of the body. Some of the causes for imbalances include antibiotics and excessive sugar intake over time. Many people who were not breast feed adequately after birth, can also have a higher risk of suffering from Candida (yeast problems), which is related to excess sugar intake in the body. People with family members suffering from diabetes should definitely consider the importance of this survey to reduce their risk of the disease. Furthermore, it is important to understand that people who have been on any fad diets or have used diet aids of any kind are at greater risk to carbohydrate sensitivity.

If you score high on this survey, you will want to strictly adhere to a balanced *Trinity Diet* program. It is also important that you seek further evaluation and intake of quality nutrients for optimizing cellular absorption of insulin and glucose. You can contact your local health professional to evaluate your BMR and then determine your specific calorie intake and supplement needs.

Date: _____

Place a check next to each statement that holds true for you.

(5) _____ I have a tendency to higher blood pressure.

(5) _____ I gain weight easily, especially around my waist and have difficulty losing it.

(5) _____ I often experience mental confusion.

(5) _____ I often experience fatigue and generalized weakness.

(10) _____ I have diabetic tendencies.

(4) _____ I get tired and/or hungry in the mid-afternoon.

(5) _____ About an hour or two after eating a full meal that includes dessert, I want more of the dessert.

(3) _____ It is harder for me to control my eating for the rest of the day if I have a breakfast containing carbohydrates than it would be if I had only coffee or nothing at all.

(4) _____ When I want to lose weight, I find it easier not to eat for most of the day than to try to eat several small diet meals.

(3) _____ Once I start eating sweets, starches, or snack foods, I often have a difficult time stopping.

(3) _____ I would rather have an ordinary meal that included dessert than a gourmet meal that did not include dessert.

(5) _____ After finishing a full meal, I sometimes feel as if I could go back and eat the whole meal again.

(3) _____ A meal of only meat and vegetables leaves me feeling unsatisfied.

(3) _____ If I'm feeling down, a snack of cake or cookies makes me feel better.

(3) _____ If potatoes, bread, pasta, or dessert are on the table, I will often skip eating vegetables or salad.

(4) _____ I get a sleepy, almost "drugged" feeling after eating a large meal containing bread or pasta or potatoes and dessert, whereas I feel more energetic after a meal of only meat or fish and salad.

(3) _____ I have a hard time going to sleep at times without a bedtime snack.

(3) _____ At times I wake in the middle of the night and can't go back to sleep unless I eat something.

(5) _____ I get irritable if I miss a meal or mealtime is delayed.

(2) _____ At a restaurant, I almost always eat too much bread, even before the meal is served.

Now add up the numbers to the left of the statements by which you placed a check, write in your total, and check your results below.

_____Total

1 to 10 You have a mild carbohydrate sensitivity. You have more freedom to eat a higher carbohydrate diet, but you still will want to follow the trinity diet.

11 to 20 You have a moderate carbohydrate sensitivity and should follow the trinity diet closely to return to optimal health.

25 or more You have a severe carbohydrate sensitivity and should follow a strict trinity diet balance to reduce disease risk. You should also consider serious supplementation support to allow for repair of depleted body systems.

CHAPTER 5

FAT: THE OIL OF
THE HOLY SPIRIT

"You love what is right and hate what is wrong. Therefore God, your God, has anointed you, pouring out the oil of joy on you more than on anyone else."
HEBREWS 1:9

THE THIRD member of *The Trinity Diet* is fats and oils. We cannot live a life of abundance in our bodies without the proper fats and oils in our choice of foods. The scriptures about the oil of joy, or the Holy Spirit, can be related to the role oil has in our health and well-being. Romans 14:17 says, "*For the kingdom of God is...righteousness, and peace, and joy in the Holy Ghost.*"

There is an irrefutable connection between the Holy Spirit and oils or fats. Essential fats are just that—essential; they are absolutely necessary for every cell membrane in the body for the purpose of good communication between the cells. Just as the Holy Spirit enables us to communicate with the Father in heaven, the oils in our body enable our cells to talk to one another. Cellular genetic information cannot be sent throughout the body efficiently, if the cell membranes do not have adequate essential fats. If you think of the cell function in your body sort of like an engine, the oil is what gives the cells the lubrication they need to function properly. You would never run an engine without oil, at least not without detrimental effects, and the same holds true for your cells.

Every cell in the human body, from nerve cells and muscle cells to brain cells, is covered with essential fatty acids (EFAs, also called omega oils or lipids). EFAs act as bonding elements that keep every cell in the body in a fluid state, empowering them to send and receive signals from hormones and enzymes. These signals enable cells to respond to and perform various functions. Without essential fats, every part of our bodies will become dysfunctional leading eventually to destruction.

As I've studied the Holy Spirit over the years, I've learned He is a sort of transmitter too. He transmits a signal from the Father to us, equipping us to respond and perform the many acts that are part of our daily walk with Him. The Lord desires us to communicate with Him, to receive His Word through the Holy Spirit, and to know His perfect will for our lives. Jesus said, *"My sheep hear my voice, and I know them, and they follow me"* (John 10:27). Jesus is referring to hearing His voice through the Holy Spirit that lives in us. Likewise, oils enable our cells to receive the information they need in order to do what they're supposed to do.

Oil is used throughout the Bible to represent the Holy Spirit. King David was anointed with oil as a symbol of the Holy Spirit confirming his call as king. You also have a calling that is just as important to God as King David's. In Jeremiah 29:11, the Lord states, *"'For I know the plans I have for you,' declares the LORD, 'plans to prosper you and not to harm you, plans to give you hope and a future.'"* Assimilating the appropriate oils and fats into your diet will assist you to walk in that plan of hope.

I remember hearing about the Holy Spirit when I was newly born again in 1986. My heart desired to know more about Him, so I spent many hours searching for truth about the Spirit of God, reading books and even taking a class at a Bible college. In the same way, during the last twenty-six years of searching for truth in health, I have found that fats and oils have been one of my greatest passions.

Jesus Feeds Fish to Thousands

One of the best sources for healthy fats and oils, is cold-water fish that are highly concentrated in EFAs. EFAs have a variety of important health benefits and include eicosapentanoic acid EPA and docosahexaenoic acid (DHA), both of which come from fish and are rich in omega-3 EFAs. The benefits of EFAs include aiding in brain function, support for health and memory, and the control of inflammation and pain in the body. Even baby formulas and prenatal vitamins are adding DHA to help brain development in children. When Jesus fed the multitudes with fish, I believe He had a specific reason for doing so. He could have really impressed the crowd by serving filet mignon. Instead however, by feeding them the fatty nutrients inherent in fish before He began to preach, Jesus better equipped their minds to comprehend His message. Not only are these benefits well known to the Creator, but they are also now widely recognized by nearly all professionals in the health and medical field. This includes traditional doctors who recommend fish oils for different diseases. In our clinic, every menu plan we use includes therapeutic concentrations of omega fatty acids.

Trinity of Essential Oils

I believe fish oil, fax oil and olive oil are the healthiest oils for the human body. Below is an overview of the benefits of each oil, as well as helpful information on selecting quality products.

Fish Oil

Fish oil is found in its highest concentration in fresh, wild cold-water fish. The EPA and DHA components of fish oil have been found to:

- Support signaling pathways within all cells
- Improve receptor sensitivity of hormones and cell messengers
- Reduce pain and inflammation through the manufacturing of anti-inflammatory hormones called prostaglandins
- Support healthy gene expression
- Thin the blood
- Improve membrane fluidity, which allows for better transfer of nutrients in and out of the cell membrane.

It is extremely important to select quality fish oils that are carefully steam distilled to extract the oils safely from the source. The majority of commercial companies that are providing fish oils today use chemicals to extract the oil from the fish. These chemicals are similar to those used in converting crude oil to gasoline and the byproducts in these fish oils add more toxins to the body doing more harm than good. In addition to using a molecular distillation process to extract oils, quality professional companies also test for heavy metals such as mercury, PCB's and other environmental toxins. These can accumulate in fish and can cause illnesses, from cancer to Alzheimer's disease. Seeking out quality professional supplement companies will protect your health investment. When selecting a quality fish oil you will want to make sure of the following:

- Check that the fish was caught in the wild or raised on a farm that does not use polychlorinated biphenyl (PCB) in their fish food.
- Verify that the fish oil was produced in Norwegian manufacturing plants that utilized the Norwegian Medicines Agency (equivalent to the FDA) for its standards.
- The fish oil should be approved by the Global Organization for EPA DHA (GOED), which was founded by experts in the field of omega-3 fatty acids.
- The product should be tested to be free of mercury, lead, dioxins, PCBs, yeasts, molds, and bacteria.

Flax Oil

Oil that is cold pressed from the flax seed is the richest plant source of omega-3 fatty acids and can provide the same benefits as fish oil if an adequate amount is consumed. Omega-3 fats are known for their cell membrane support, production of hormones, and inflammation control. They are broken down to DHA and EPA by a healthy functioning liver. From EPA, your body makes hormones called prostaglandins (PGs) that control pain and inflammation. Medication, chemicals, food additives, caffeine and many synthetic food chemicals can block your body's ability to produce healthy PG. Therefore it is important to be sure your organs are functioning properly in order to fully realize the benefits of omega-3 fats. Chapter seven provides in-depth information on how to improve the cleansing actions of your body. The removal of environmental toxins from our bodies is an essential function that must be supported for the natural control of pain and inflammation. For many years, my body was wracked with pain and I thought drugs were the only answer. Later, I learned that medication only contributed to the increased level of pain. Today, with the proper intake of essential fats, I do not use medication for anything, including pain.

Another factor that can interfere with your body's ability to assimilate omega-3 fatty acids is the excess consumption of processed, heated, or hydrogenated oils. When the body expends its energy to rid itself of toxins from processed oils, the omega-3 fatty oils you do consume can become compromised, interfering with optimal cellular function.

Flax oil is very unstable and must be refrigerated. Do not heat fax oil as it will hydrogenate, which can damage cellular tissue due to free radical oxidation.

Olive Oil

The benefits of olive oil result from the many naturally occurring molecules in the extra virgin unrefined oil. We dedicate the following extensive list of benefits to the Lord because this oil is referenced in the scriptures 74 times. The quality of olive oil:

- Helps improve brain cell maturation
- Lowers the amount of circulating cholesterol
- Reduces gallstone formation
- Improves fat digestion
- Aids in elimination of materials from the liver (liver detoxification)
- Increases bile excretion
- Stimulates pancreatic enzyme production
- Facilitates membrane development
- Decreases cholesterol absorption from food

Olive oil is available as refined and extra virgin. I always encourage purchasing oil that is most like its original state. A dark green oil, protected in dark glass or in a can, will prevent light from increasing any oxidation of the oil. If the heat is not excessive, olive oil will remain stable when heated due to the mono-unsaturated fatty acids present in the oil. Excessive heat in a hot skillet or pan can cause oxidation and be detrimental to any oil, so always put oil in the pan before cooking and slowly bring up the heat. Add the food soon after the oil is properly heated. Heat is damaging to any food and must be controlled so that foods do not lose valuable nutrition.

Good Fat vs. Bad Fat

Researchers have falsely declared that excessive dietary fats are the major cause of obesity, heart disease, cancer and autoimmune disorders, such as diabetes and arthritis. They now link it to many brain and neurological problems as well. Researchers presume that *any* dietary fats are the cause of increased disease, throwing the good in with the bad. Because of ignorance, there is still tremendous fear and confusion in the general public about whether to consume even the good fats, better known as essential fats. This confusion and fear remains largely due to the greed and lies that permeate the U.S. processed food industry and the Food and Drug Administration (FDA). In fact, many of the toxic oils found in margarine, shortenings, salad dressings, baked goods, chocolate, ice cream, potato chips, candy and snack foods are illegal in European countries where great care is taken to insure food is delivered in its most health-promoting state. When you compare food labels between American and European products, you can see the difference. Have you ever eaten pure Swiss chocolate? What an amazing food! If you compare its label with an American made chocolate—full of chemicals and hydrogenated oils, you'll discover that there are many more synthetic chemicals in American chocolate. Our Swiss friends bring us the best quality chocolates in the world! Europeans even use a different process to mill the chocolate, so that it does not irritate the digestive tract.

The fact is, all oils are not evil, yet people get upset with me and say, "But isn't the oil fat?" Yes. It is called fat, but essential oils are the fat every cell in the human body requires to perform more than five thousand chemical reactions every second of the day. Every cell in the body is covered with fat! If the cell becomes diminished in fatty acids, its communication and function becomes disturbed—even to the point of disease.

A woman named Mildred came into our office shaking from head to foot from Parkinson's disease. Knowing EFA intake is beneficial for nerve function, I knew it would help enable her body to repair. I gave her 36 grams of flax seed oil and fish oil per day. After only one week of high concentrations of EFAs, she stopped shaking. At age 84, after just one week on *The Trinity Diet*, she returned to her doctor, who was quite surprised and said, "You don't have Parkinson's disease anymore. I don't know what you have." Many years later, she experienced more health issues and her family chose to seek help from physicians who prescribed medication. Soon after, she passed away. Many people unknowingly compromise their quality and length of life or that of a loved one, when they seek answers in medicine rather than the Lord. Near death at age 84, if Mildred's family would not have given into the use of medication, I believe they could have helped her live an even longer and more abundant life.

The Danger of Toxic Refined Oils

In order to know the truth, that it may set you free, there has to be solid teaching. There really has not been enough education on the topic of fat for God's people to know the truth. The Bible actually instructs us on fat intake in Leviticus 3:17, where God said not to eat of the fat of animals—most scientists would agree that this is bad for your health. This fat is known as saturated fat. Another unhealthy fat is trans fats, or hydrogenated fats. These are fats and oils that come from plants, but are damaged and de-natured during heat processing or cooking. These have been found to be more damaging to our health than even animal fat.

Sadly, people today consume excessive amounts of processed fats, some fifty times more than people did in the early nineteen hundreds. The consumption of toxic oils was nearly non-existent in the beginning of the twentieth century, as were the diseases of fatty degeneration such as diabetes, heart disease, cancer and arthritis.

Hydrogenated oils cause a multitude of health problems, including:

- Elevated LDL "bad" cholesterol levels
- Decreased HDL "good" cholesterol levels
- Increased risk of cancer, heart disease, fertility problems, auto-immune disease and bone degeneration
- Inhibited insulin receptors in cell membranes, which are the main cause of type 2 diabetes, which is characterized by high levels of insulin and glucose in the blood.

Gary is an out-of-town client of mine who called me very upset. He had visited a doctor who had heard an irregularity during his heart examination and wanted to run a number of exams. In Gary's words, they wanted to "make a mountain out of a molehill." Gary is seventy-three years old, does not consume medication and exercises multiple times per week. He takes supplements to support his food intake and gets plenty of rest and relaxation. There was no evidence that his heart was restricted, as his resting pulse rate was very low due to his years of exercise. It was clear to me that he did not have heart disease. He wanted to know what to do.

We decided to perform a blood spot fatty acid test to determine the balance of omega fats in his blood and to see if there were excess amounts of trans-fats in the blood. We mailed the test kit to Gary, he performed a finger prick in his home, and he sent the test strip to the lab for testing. The test results showed Gary had an excellent balance of omega-3 fats, DHA and EPA, and all his nutritional fats were in balance. However, his test showed he was off the chart in trans-fatty acids. With careful research, we were able to identify that he was consuming trans-fats from oils in a particular salad dressing he used. The oil was a vegetable oil with soybean and sunflower oils in it. This salad dressing was probably heat processed; therefore, these poly-unsaturated plant oils became a toxic trans-fat. Gary has since eliminated processed vegetable oils from his diet and has no issues with his heart. Gary is my father and is another example of living an abundant, healthy life without the use of medication at age seventy-four.

With all the advances in knowledge with regards to healthy fats found in fish and vegetation, most people do not understand the difference between the types of fats. They believe that all fat is bad for your body, which is why sales of "low fat" and fat free" products have skyrocketed in recent years. When I read the packaging on food in the grocery, and it claims "low fat" or "fat free," I stay away. Just because a product is labeled low-fat does not make it healthy. Also, a lack of essential fats can actually cause the very conditions that are caused by consuming bad fats.

The best foods to choose are whole foods and those with the fewest chemical names on the labels. An excellent resource for a deeper understanding of the guidelines for identifying good and bad oils in labels and food is *Fats that Heal, Fats that Kill* by Udo Erasmus. This is a serious topic that is a bit complicated, and Erasmus' book will help you with a practical understanding you can apply in your everyday food choices. As a general rule, when evaluating packaged foods, search the labels and stay away from hydrogenated or partially hydrogenated oils. Any oil that is heat processed and is polyunsaturated oil will become a trans fat that is toxic to human health. Many products will say they are free of trans fat, but when you look closely, you will see that they have used a polyunsaturated vegetable oil of some kind — sunflower, safflower, etc. When these oils are heated they become trans fats.

This is the result of sheer ignorance on the part of manufacturers who are so focused on the bottom line, that they have lost track of consumers' health.

When we do find beneficial foods with good oils, we are giving our bodies the critical EFAs we need to protect the genetic material in our cells from damage caused by toxic chemicals in the environment. This protection is the most effective means for preventing the diseases of fatty degeneration such as cancer, heart disease, diabetes and arthritis.

Adequate Fat and Weight Loss

One question people frequently ask me is: "Won't consuming essential fats contribute to ugly body fat?" The answer is no!

Betty came to my office wanting to improve a variety of health issues. Her metabolic rate was 1450, which meant she burned 1,450 calories at rest in a twenty-four hour period. This is a fairly good calorie burn level for a woman who is five feet eight inches tall. While mainstream reasoning would have told her to reduce her calorie intake, I started her on a food program of roughly 2,000 calories per day, some 500 calories more than her body was burning in a day at that time. Approximately 800 calories of her daily caloric intake was from fats and oils, such as flax seed oil and olive oil. After ten days on the program, she lost six pounds of toxic fat and excess water weight. More importantly, the conversion happened at the cellular level, which allowed her body to increase metabolism.

Increasing oils to 20 percent or more in your *Trinity Diet* will cause your cell energy to increase, therefore burning more calories. You will observe additional benefits by removing toxic saturated fats and hydrogenated oils from the body. If you make essential oils as mandatory to physical health as the Holy Spirit is to spiritual health, every cell of your body will enjoy abundant health.

Cholesterol: Bad Guy or Lie?

Cholesterol is a fatty sterol found in animal fats. It has been targeted as the "bad guy" of a wide range of health issues, but let's look at some little-known facts about cholesterol.

- Cholesterol is distributed in the body, especially in the bile, skin, blood, brain tissue, liver, kidneys, adrenal glands, and myelin sheaths or nerve fibers.
- Cholesterol facilitates the absorption and transport of fatty acids and helps facilitate the synthesis of vitamin D at the surface of the skin.

This vitamin can be converted into steroid hormones in the body to repair and rebuild cellular tissues.

- Your body is able to make 20,000 I.U. of vitamin D from cholesterol in just twenty minutes of sun exposure.
- Cholesterol is needed to create various steroid hormones such as cortisol, and aldosterone in the adrenal glands. These hormones suppress inflammation reactions and regulate water balance.
- Cholesterol is involved in the synthesis of the sex hormones progesterone, estrogen and testosterone.
- Cholesterol assists in preventing skin infections and helps the healing process.
- Cholesterol functions as an antioxidant, especially when other antioxidants are low or unavailable.

Cholesterol exists naturally in all animal tissues, including in those of humans. It is synthesized in the body, primarily in the liver and adrenal glands. The more cholesterol we eat, the less our body needs to create. The less we eat, the more our body will manufacture. Just like fats, we have not been educated in the difference between natural cholesterol and oxidized cholesterol. Back in the nineteen seventies, studies that correlated blood cholesterol levels with increased incidents of cardiovascular disease were performed with oxidized cholesterol. Oxidized cholesterol is created when cholesterol is overheated or damaged with oxidation during excess processing and cooking. Research has found that oxidized cholesterol, not cholesterol that is naturally produced in our bodies, appears to be the greater factor in arterial disease.

It is possible to reverse heart disease by following *The Trinity Diet* and the following nutritional guidelines:

- Consume antioxidant nutrients such as vitamins A, C, D, E, B_3, selenium and chromium.
- Obtain sufficient essential fatty acids from nuts, seeds, and cold processed oils.
- Eat a high-fiber diet of forty to fifty grams daily.
- Avoid over-processed animal fats, hydrogenated fats, trans- fats and altered oils.
- Follow a *Trinity Diet* consisting of unrefined, unprocessed, whole, organically grown plant-based foods.

- Engage regularly in cardiovascular exercise to strengthen the heart muscle.

In fact, even a *Journal of the American Medical Association* study as far back as November 1, 1995, found that cardiac arrest (heart attack) can be reduced up to ninety percent with optimal intake of omega-3 fatty acids (oils) found in fish, fax and other oils.[2] So finally the doctors are now recommending fish oil for heart health.

Meds vs. EFAs

Medicines treat pain by masking, burying or removing symptoms. Because medications shut off the very symptoms God designed to initiate healing and repair, further destruction to the body is inevitable. In addition, drugs cause many diseases themselves by disrupting the delicate design of our body and the life-sustaining functions the Lord created in each one of us.

As the Holy Spirit is our comforter, easing our pain and suffering, so essential oils control pain naturally by providing the building blocks for specific hormones which control pain in the body, such as prostaglandins. These fatty acids are short lived, so just like we must continuously be in fellowship with the Spirit—to enjoy the benefits of His presence, we must regularly consume fatty acids that produce hormones and control pain. They are as essential to physical health as the constant comfort and counsel from the Holy Spirit is to spiritual health. Moreover, as the Holy Spirit will keep us from trouble and destruction, we have seen many frustrating symptoms and diseases reversed with the simple intake of these essential oils.

For example, Bobby Wilson, a fifty-three-year-old friend of mine who is a professional golfer, was suffering from chronic knee pain due to a previous injury. Rather than take medication, Bobby chose to take an extra-strength EPA/DHA fish oil from our Nutrition and Health Center. After taking 6,000 to 8,000 milligrams of EPA-rich fish oil for just one

[2] Siscovick, D.; Raghunathan, T.; King, I.; Weinmann, S.; Wicklund, K.; Albright, J.; Bovbjerg, V.; Arbogast, P.; Smith, H.; Kushi, L. (November 1, 1995). Dietary intake and cell membrane levels of long-chain n-3 polyunsaturated fatty acids and the risk of primary cardiac arrest. Journal of the American Medical Association, Vol. 274 (No. 17).

month, his pain level went from a ten to about a four, and he was able to continue to work on his long drive—golf skills. In the winter, Bobby set a world record of winning two back-to-back titles as senior and super senior world champion long driver. Congratulations, Bobby, for your diligence in taking care of your body and your long deserved road to success!

Many women find that the inflammation which causes hot flashes completely disappears with adequate intake of EFAs. We have seen diabetic patients lower their glucose numbers and begin to require little or no medication due to adequate fatty acid intake. We have also noted a reversal of artery plaque, as well as lower blood pressure, in patients with an increase of EFA intake. These examples of healing, glorify God who created our bodies for regeneration. As people learn to live a more abundant life by consuming more EFAs, the testimonies of healing will continue.

Sources of Essential Fats

In the nineteen hundreds, the average consumption of omega 6 fat from vegetable oil was one pound per year. Just one century later, the average American consumes seventy-five pounds of omega 6 fats per year. Some of the omega 6 oils are soy, safflower, sunflower, and corn. As we discussed earlier, inflammation in the body is kept under control by prostaglandins (PGs) that are manufactured from quality oils, most of which are the omega-3 type. This excess intake of omega 6 oils, especially in a processed state, is a serious health threat as it aggravates the very inflammation that is the foundation for most all diseases.

Choosing the right fats is critical to your health. Below is a chart that shows the sources of essential and non-essential fats. The numbers in each column represent the percentage of fatty acids found in each oil. Oils that have high amounts of omega-3 fatty acids are the most excellent choice. Oils that have high concentrations of omega 6, mono- unsaturated and saturated fats, should be avoided.

Cold-Pressed Oils

Cold-pressed oils cannot be heated. Their natural state becomes altered, and they can damage cell membranes. They must be used in their natural, unaltered state in order for the body to realize their intended benefits. Unfortunately, when found in commercially processed foods, most of these products have been hydrogenated from heat processing, which creates trans fats that have been linked to a higher rate of inflammation and disease.

FOOD SOURCE	OMEGA 3 POLY LINOLENIC ACID	OMEGA 6 POLY LINOLEIC ACID	MONO- UNSATURATED	SATURATED
FLAXSEED	54	15	22	9
PUMPKIN SEED	15	45	32	8
SOYBEAN	11	42	32	15
WALNUT	5	50	29	16
SAFFLOWER	-	70	18	12
SUNFLOWER	-	66	22	12
CORN	-	59	25	16
SESAME	-	45	45	13
RICE BRAN	-	35	48	17

Safer Cooking Oils

These oils do not de-nature under heat and are the best choices for cooking. My preference is olive oil, as it is referenced more than seventy times in the Bible.

Oils to Avoid

These oils are NOT recommended for any use.

FOOD SOURCE	OMEGA 3 POLY LINOLENIC ACID	OMEGA 6 POLY LINOLEIC	MONO- UNSATURATED	SATURATED
PEANUT (CONTAINS CARCINOGENS)	-	29	56	15
COTTONSEED (MAY CONTAIN TOXINS)	-	48	28	24
PALM	-	9	44	48
PALM KERNEL	-	2	18	80

Your Body: A Temple

The temple of God in the Old Testament was the physical earthly location where the Lord's presence would manifest—but where is God's temple today? According to 1 Corinthians 6:19 (NASB), our bodies are now the temples of God. It says, *"Or do you not know that your body is a temple of the Holy Spirit who is in you, whom you have from God, and that you are not your own? For you have been bought with a price: therefore glorify God in your body."* Under the new covenant, by the blood of Christ Jesus shed on the cross for our sins, we are the temples of the Holy Spirit. Each day, the most important thing we can do is spend time with the Holy Spirit to allow Him to change us into the image of Christ.

Before moving on to the next chapter or your next task, take a few moments to quiet yourself and pray this short prayer:

> Lord God of all creation, I ask You to send Your Holy Spirit in power today to help me to change and become obedient to Your Word. I know You desire me to be abundantly healthy. Father, help me to be an example in my body, the temple of Your Holy Spirit. Use me as a light so that others will see You in me and give glory to You. Come and show me how You can heal me more every day, as You restore me to health. In Jesus' name, Amen.

Yes, you can line your life up with the word of God and walk in perfect health. By consuming an adequate amount of essential fats and refusing to consume hydrogenated oil and saturated animal fats, you can live a longer, more abundant life to the glory of God. As your cells properly function and communicate, you will have the opportunity to realize God's full design for your life, and you can become a truly healthy child of God. At the end of chapter ten, there is a *Checklist of a Healthy Human* you can use to determine how healthy you really are. Take the test now, and then retake it after implementing *The Trinity Diet* for three to six months. The results may surprise you.

CHAPTER 6

THE SOURCE OF
SICKNESS

"If you will listen carefully to the voice of the LORD your God
and do what is right in his sight, obeying his commands and
laws, then I will not make you suffer the diseases I sent on
the Egyptians; for I am the LORD who heals you."
EXODUS 15:26 (NLT)

I F ABUNDANT health is God's plan for us, then why do we get sick?
Let's go deeper to comprehend why disease is so common among
Christians today and what you can do to reverse disease!

There are three principal causes of disease: trauma, toxicity and
insufficiency.

Trauma

Many diseases are precipitated by trauma. Emotional trauma might
result from the death of a spouse, divorce, abuse, financial loss due to
fire, food, etc. Electromagnetic trauma would include things like high
voltage power lines, computers, cellular phones, televisions, etc. Physical
trauma might occur due to car accidents, falls, birth trauma, sports
injuries, etc.

Numerous people have come to my office suffering from disease
linked to trauma. Most recently, I have seen an influx of clients affected
by a category four hurricane that hit the Houston area. People's lives were
turned upside down, and many of them lost their homes. This type of
trauma takes a terrible toll on the body. The physical demands required
of the body to repair itself from trauma, put most people in a catch-up-
to-repair mode. Many times, the rebuilding and repairing process can be

extended for years unnecessarily, due to poor lifestyle choices. However, if additional nutrients are taken during times of trauma, when stress may cause a breakdown in the body, they will help counteract any resulting adverse effects.

Toxicity

Clinical nutritionists and naturopaths agree toxicity is the major cause of degenerative diseases today. Synthetic or man-made materials can be very toxic causing a cascade of damaging effects to cellular function in all parts of the body. There are tens of thousands of synthetic chemicals influencing our bodies every day. In the United States, billions of pounds of toxic chemicals are released into the environment each year. These include paint cleaners, solvents, perfumes, fuel, pesticides, fungicides, herbicides, and synthetic hormones found in plastics. It is estimated that the average American has more than two hundred toxic chemicals in their blood at any given time.

Remember the Bible says that the blood is the life of the flesh. With our blood so contaminated with chemicals, how could one focus on a spiritual battle that requires a healthy body? Our battle on the physical front involves knowing the sources of toxicity and how to best defend our bodies from them. Food, skin care products, cleaners, pesticides, and synthetic clothes are some of the major sources of these poisonous toxins. Our organic bodies do not function well with toxic interference.

Additionally, toxic microbes, like parasites, viruses, bacteria, fungus, mold, and yeast are among the many known invading organisms that are pathogenic in the body. Derived from the Greek meaning "that which produces suffering," a pathogen is a biological agent that causes disease or illness to the host. We are particularly susceptible to these pathogens due to the overuse of antibiotics that damage and reduce the protective bacteria in the intestines. This good bacteria is one of our body's most powerful defenses against disease. Without it, there is ample room for the overgrowth of bad bacteria, yeast and parasites.

It is estimated that in a single day, U.S. citizens alone, ingest somewhere between one hundred thousand to ten million foreign bacteria into their digestive systems.[3] Fortunately, the Lord has made many natural and herbal remedies that have anti-bacterial, anti-fungal and anti-parasitic benefits. Some of the most powerful include oregano, thyme, lemon balm, wormwood, and pau d'arco. Although natural remedies were here first, some call their use *alternative* medicine, when actually, chemical-based symptom relievers such as medications and pharmakeia—as the scripture calls it, should be called the alternative. (See *Chapter Eight* for more information and useful ideas on the many benefits of herbal remedies.)

Insufficiency

Health issues abound from insufficiencies in a number of areas including nutrition, air quality and sleep. By understanding the different and most common deficiencies, you can begin to make key adjustments in your lifestyle that will bring great benefit to your health and quality of life.

Nutrients and Supplements

In 2 Corinthians 9:8, the Bible says, *"And God is able to make all grace abound to you, so that always having all sufficiency in everything, you may have an abundance for every good deed."* God's intention is that we would always be sufficient in all things, yet we are still sick, weak, overweight and unmotivated because the standard diet lacks the nutrients we need.

If you are sowing the right seed of natural foods into your body, you will not be deficient. Unfortunately, this is not the case for most people today. Even the recommended daily allowance (RDA), that was developed more than forty years ago, is not met in the diet of more than 70 percent of all Americans. This is unfortunate, considering that the RDA is an inadequate amount of nutrients.

The lack of nutrients or insufficiency in our diets today comes from our over-consumption of processed foods that hold little to no nutritional value. In 2 Corinthians 9, the Lord explains that the reason we lack, is because we have failed to sow adequately to receive the harvest that

---

[3] Jaffe, R. (MD, phD,). Presentation. International and American Association of Clinical Nutritionists Sept 2007 Orlando Florida

is needed. The absence of vibrant health in the body of Christ today is evidence that we have not sown sufficiently into our bodies. Amy and I have witnessed clients drive up to our office in very expensive automobiles, yet they say they can't afford to eat healthy and take quality supplements. They have misplaced their priorities in life. In Galatians 6:7, we are told, *"Do not be deceived: God cannot be mocked. A man reaps what he sows."* The more we sow the more harvest we will reap. Therefore, I always recommend a serious quality professional supplement program based on a person's individual chemistry to sow abundant nutrients into the soil of the body.

Ten years ago, only 10 percent of doctors believed that supplements were important. Now, more than 90 percent of doctors will agree that supplements provide a necessary benefit to health. Taking quality supplements is one way you can make up for the inadequacy of nutrients in your diet, and it is an excellent way to sow good health into your body.

Amy and I knew when we committed to take care of our bodies that God was going to provide, because it is His will for us to be healthy. We economized in every other area of our life so we could do just that. I gave up golf for a season in my life because it was just too expensive (and if you knew how much I love golf, you would understand that sacrifice). We rarely ate out at restaurants, and Amy went to garage sales for our children's clothes. I assure you, investing in your health will always pay off.

Air Quality

We must also consider air quality when evaluating the sources of toxins in our immediate environment. Indoor air has been shown to be more toxic than outdoor air. This is due to chemicals that are manufactured into or are put off by products ranging from computers, plastics, carpet chemicals, paint, and indoor synthetic materials.

Outdoor air quality is a serious issue as well. The Houston area is well known for its toxic levels of pollutants, from automobiles to industrial waste. With the regular use of an indoor air purifier, you can keep your home and work place clear of these toxic chemicals and provide optimal air quality in the midst of even the most toxic cities.

When selecting an indoor air purifier, consider your specific objectives, and then talk to various air purification experts to learn about the many different types available. Certain air purifiers remove more bacteria, while others remove more heavy metals, and still others clean smoke and remove odors. You will also want to consider using ozone, ultra violet, ionic, hepa or carbon-type filters, as they all provide excellent air purifying qualities that remove toxic particles, bacteria and chemicals from the air. Regardless of what you choose, don't live indoors anywhere without a good air purification system in place. Your lungs will thank you for it.

Natural Light

Our bodies require natural sunlight for optimal mental function and for the production of vitamin D. On his website, www. VitaminDCouncil. org, Dr. John Jacob Cannell, presents an abundance of research on the relationship between low levels of vitamin D and higher risks for breast, colon, prostate and other cancers. His research has also shown that people who have been diagnosed with melanoma (skin cancer) tend to be fair skinned individuals who as a result do not go out into the sun as much. Interestingly, the locations of the melanomas are also not typically exposed to the sun. Our bodies need vitamin D from the sun, and that's one of the reasons Amy and I have a year-round tan. We are careful to receive regular sunlight to optimize our vitamin D levels. Another benefit of vitamin D from the sun is that it increases hormones in the body that repair, restore, and strengthen weak fingernails and bones.[4]

As mentioned previously, if you spend between twenty minutes and up to an hour a day in the sunshine your body can produce up to 20,000 I.U. of vitamin D from the cholesterol in your skin. While a supplement of cod liver oil may only deliver 400 I.U. of vitamin D, the sun provides a more economical source. Since the average American spends most of their life indoors, it is no wonder that we have a cholesterol problem, not to mention a depression problem!

Sleep

Most people I meet are so stressed that they have trouble falling asleep, and most only receive six hours of sleep on any given night. This creates problems because it is only during deep rapid eye movement

---

[4] Sunshine: You can learn of the abundance of health benefits provided by the sun from lowering cancer risks to reduced bone fracture risks at: www.vitamindcouncil.com.

(REM) sleep that our bodies produce growth hormones for the repair of damage to tissue throughout the day. Inadequate sleep can cause adrenal fatigue, bags under the eyes, blood sugar imbalances, and pain and inflammation in the body. Naturopath wisdom of the ages shows that adults need seven to eight hours of quality sleep each night to restore and repair from the day. Sleeping less than seven hours per night increases the risk of mortality in both men and women.[5]

The Trinity of the Disease Process

As we've seen, our bodies reflect the triune nature of God. There is also a three-fold process to developing disease in the body. First, the body constantly works to excrete the accumulation of toxic waste. Unable to remove incoming toxins at a quick enough rate, it begins to deposit them into the internal tissues, organs, fluid compartments and fat tissue. Finally, when there is an excessive accumulation of toxins, the body begins to break down, and degeneration and disease begins.

The great news is that no matter where you are in the process of degeneration, the body is able to remove toxins and move toward healing. God has designed our bodies to reverse the course of disease and return to abundant health. This differs greatly from what our society has been told about disease being linked to certain genetic risks. History tells us different. Has anyone ever asked you what your ancestors died of in the early nineteen hundreds before packaged food was introduced? Are you aware that only 3 percent of people died from cancer at that time versus the 50 percent who die from cancer today? There is much deception in the world today concerning our health, and one of the greatest lies is that disease is genetic.

According to God's word, I believe we all have the genetic potential to be extremely healthy like Jack LaLanne at age ninety-five or Moses who died when he was one hundred and twenty years old. Yet medicine in our world today focuses almost exclusively on the disease process, and society as a whole has almost completely ignored the process of healing and restoration found in each one of us—just as they have ignored the Creator.

---

[5] Sleep and Mortality: A Population-Based 22-Year Follow-Up Study. Journal SLEEP. Vol 30. No. 10. 1245-1253.

Many Christians in these last days are falling into the distraction of crisis care as medical focus moves more and more to relieving symptoms rather than truly getting to the root cause of the dysfunction or disease. With toxic chemicals in the environment and fast foods on the rise, the cause of health problems is apparent. However, despite the vast array of new medical technologies, people are still having difficulty healing. It is helpful to know that symptoms such as fever or pain are signals from the body to initiate healing and change.

Let's say, for example, you accidentally place your hand on a hot stove. Almost immediately, your autonomic nervous system responds telling you to quickly remove your hand before you even have time to think. But what would happen to your hand if you had taken a painkiller to deaden the nerve endings? If you couldn't feel the pain, you wouldn't remove your hand until you actually smelled burning flesh or saw your hand burning. This is exactly what medication does to cover up the symptoms God designed to protect and repair our body. Pain is the signal that tells us something is wrong and guides us to the root of the problem.

If you are someone who has been diagnosed with disease, I understand. I have been there. If you are hearing words that label you as a victim of chance, stop and listen for the voice of restoration. If you ask God, as I did, a door will open for Him to do more than you can ask or imagine. I pray that He will show you that you are a walking miracle of His designed healing.

In his letter to the Philippians, Paul says, *"I can do all things through Christ which strengthens me" (4:13)*. With the over-committed, over-burdened lifestyle most Americans embrace, it is hard to remember to listen to the strong and steady voice that reminds us to be faithful and hopeful. It is this voice that guards us from the condemnation of the accuser—the one who talks of suffering and death. Hebrews 11:1 tells us, *"Now faith is the substance of things hoped for and the evidence of things not seen."* Maybe it is time to evaluate your faith. James 2:18 challenges us, *"You have faith, and I have works. Show me your faith without your works, and I will show you my faith by my works."*

Do you have faith to believe that God will deliver you from disease? Are you doing something about it or just expecting God to do it? It says in 2 Chronicles 16:12 that *"King Asa was diseased in his feet; though the disease was great he did not seek the Lord but the physicians."* In the next verse, the Bible tells us he died.

Because I chose to obey the Lord's directive spoken in my heart saying, "Seek out a way; there is a way," I was able to avoid a life of therapy, medication, and possibly decades in a wheelchair. I can tell you from experience, God makes a way where there seems to be no way. Isaiah 43:18 tells us, *"Do not call to mind the former things, or ponder things of the past. Behold, I will do something new, now it will spring forth; will you not be aware of it? I will even make a roadway in the wilderness, rivers in the desert."* Unlike King Asa, because I obeyed, sought, and applied God's principles, I am living in abundant health.

I believe that He will do this for you as well, but it will require change. All it takes is a mindset that you are just going do it. Live life, but live it differently than you have before. Ask the Lord, seek out His way, keep knocking and searching with all your heart. Search for wisdom more than silver and gold.

May we honor God by listening to the Holy Spirit in times of affliction, to find our way back to health without medication— pharmakiea, to cover up the pain. Isaiah 40:31 says, *"But they that wait upon the LORD shall renew their strength..."* The Hebrew word for *wait* means to "wait eagerly for or linger." This means that there is an expectation that God will pull through and show us He is who He says He is—Jehovah Rophe, our healer. Because we are partners with God, our faith will produce actions that enable healing as well. How you respond to stress and disease in your life will truly bring out the depth of your faith. As the struggling, sinful and suffering King David said in Psalm 119:71, *"It was good for me to be afflicted so that I might learn your decrees."*

Waiting on God

One summer we took our children to a water park with a friend. Our daughter, Shawnna, came down one of the slides, hit her foot on the bottom of the pool, and bent it forward. Almost immediately, the top of her foot swelled, and she was in a lot of pain. Our friend's first reaction was to tell us to go directly to the emergency room. We decided to be patient and wait on God for direction. We knew that God designed our bodies to heal themselves, and with rest and proper nutrition, we believed she would be fine. We elevated her foot and iced it down. Over the next few days, we monitored Shawnna's foot and watched to see if it was getting better or growing worse. She was able to get around on crutches, and soon she could put some weight on it. Each day she improved, and before long, she was back to normal.

We are not recommending you avoid the emergency room when necessary, but this was not a life-threatening injury. Sometimes we must wait upon the Lord. We do not have to respond in fear. We can have an ear to hear His voice and listen to His words of wisdom. The Bible tells us, *"We do not want you to become lazy, but to imitate those who through faith and patience inherit what has been promised"* (Hebrews 6:12). In verse fifteen, it goes on to say, *"After waiting patiently, Abraham received what was promised."*

As believers, we know God can heal instantaneously. There is proof throughout the scriptures of Jesus healing all manner of disease and sickness on the spot. Matthew 4:24 reports, *"News about him spread all over Syria, and people brought to him all who were ill with various diseases, those suffering severe pain, the demon-possessed, those having seizures, and the paralyzed, and he healed them."*

Today many Christians unnecessarily struggle with chronic, lingering sickness and disease. As in all things, scripture provides the answer as to why many may not be receiving their healing. Take time to meditate on the following scriptures. I pray you will grasp the vision the Lord has for you to find healing, as well as the importance of your personal choices.

"...every curse has a cause" (Proverbs 26:2).

"God is not mocked, what you sow you will reap" (Galatians 6:7).

"But people who are not aware that they are doing wrong will be punished only lightly. Much is required from those to whom much is given, and much more is required from those to whom much more is given" (Luke 12:48).

If we believe God's word is true, knowing that we will reap what we sow, then there is no way we can put lifeless food into our bodies and expect to be well! We are mocking God. He has given us clear instruction on how to feed our bodies, yet we continue to think we can eat whatever we want and expect good health. As Christians, we have been given the Holy Spirit to counsel us in our decisions, including what to eat. If we are truly seeking Him, we will find answers. He tells us in Jeremiah 29:13, *"When you seek me you will find me when you search for me with all your heart."*

Jesus said in John 10:27, *"My sheep hear my voice, and I know them, and they follow me."*

Jesus said He would give us the keys to the Kingdom. In this book, I share with you the keys the Lord has given me to help deliver my family, friends and thousands of clients from disease and needless suffering. I pray you have an ear to hear His voice.

Medical Doctor: Different Perspective

Russell M. Jaffe, MD, Ph.D., CCN, is a trusted mentor whom I have had the privilege of knowing for seventeen years. Once at an international nutrition conference, Dr. Jaffe spoke of his early days as a researcher for the National Institute of Health (NIH). After spending time at NIH studying disease, he turned to his colleagues and asked them if they had ever considered studying the mechanisms of health in the body. After his colleagues looked at him with great bewilderment, he decided he needed to pursue knowledge in wellness care, not just disease.

Dr. Jaffe has had the privilege of contributing to the "birth" of modern integrative medicine. He works from the first principles of biology to clarify the causal mechanisms of good health and ill health. He has published more than one hundred articles, and invited reviews attesting to his professional contributions. Today, Dr. Jaffe provides education, counsel, and quality nutritional supplements through his company, Perque. If you can acquire these products through a health care professional in your area, please ask for them. I have used Perque products in my practice for more than fifteen years, and I highly recommend them.

Supplementation of quality nutrients such as those provided by Dr. Jaffe are a vital part of making *The Trinity Diet* work more effectively at the cellular level. Food supplies today are lacking many important co-factors such as vitamins, minerals, enzymes and thousands of phytonutrients that can be found in quality supplementation.

Sorcery

Sorcery is a word used in the book of Revelation to warn us of things to come. In Revelation 18:23, the Lord tells us, *"And the light of a candle shall shine no more at all in thee; and the voice of the bridegroom and of the bride shall be heard no more at all in thee: for thy merchants were the great men of the earth; for by thy sorceries were all nations deceived."* This word sorcery comes from the Greek word "pharmakeia,"[6] which literally means "drugs", and appears four other times in the New Testament, Gal 5:20, Rev 9:21, 18:23, 21:8, and 22:15. "Pharmakeia" is translated into our English Bibles as either "witchcraft" or "sorcery". This is where we get our English word "pharmacy", from the Greek word "pharmakeia". In each of the these five passages, "pharmakeia", or "drugs" is listed as a work of the flesh of man, directly opposed to the Spirit of God at work in us.

Sorcery or witchcraft—pharmakeia draws us into the control of the world's system which is bondage. Yet, Jesus came to set the captives free! John 8:36 says, *"Whom the Son sets free is free indeed."* This freedom comes by way of the truth as it is revealed to those who are open to receive. In Luke 10:21, Jesus says, *"I thank you, Father, Lord of heaven and earth, that you have hidden these things from the wise and understanding and revealed them to little children; yes, Father, for such was your gracious will."*

I was once in bondage to medication and ignorant myself. It was God who gave me the wisdom and direction to set me free. I pray that you too will be set free as you read more of the healing testimonies of others, who have also been delivered from the power of pharmakeia and into His marvelous promise of abundant health.

Godliness without Power

Most people who come to our health center desperately want to be off medication. Taking medication, except perhaps in life or death emergencies, is contrary to the very nature of God and how He designed our bodies to work. Because of the stronghold of "pharmakeia" or medication, those dependent upon it do not feel free. Many come to me after being told that they will be on medication for the rest of their lives. That's not freedom. It is this system of denying God's power for the body to heal itself, that the Lord mentions in 2 Timothy 3:1-6 when he says:

---

[6] according to Strong's Exhaustive Concordance of the Bible G5331

"But mark this: There will be terrible times in the last days. People will be lovers of themselves, lovers of money, boastful, proud, abusive, disobedient to their parents, ungrateful, unholy, without love, unforgiving, slanderous, without self-control, brutal, not lovers of the good, treacherous, rash, conceited, lovers of pleasure rather than lovers of God—having a form of godliness but denying its power. Have nothing to do with them."

When we deny the healing power of Christ by accepting hopeless medical diagnoses, we are engaging in a form of godliness that denies God's power, and we are submitting to the arrogance that permeates the medical field, where physicians often are their own gods. It was this very arrogance that led me to seek the Lord for healing instead of simply following man and his ways. For more than twenty years now, my wife, our three children and I have abstained from any participation in the use of pharmakeia. We are free to heal naturally, just as our Creator intended, and you can be too.

The Woman with the Issue of Blood

Scripture offers answers to all things, even pharmakeia. Mark 5:25-26 tells the story of *"a certain woman, which had an issue of blood twelve years, and had suffered many things of many physicians, and had spent all that she had, and was nothing bettered, but rather grew worse."* This scripture reference is a remarkably accurate depiction of women and their female health issues today. When you examine these verses more closely, you find that the woman had an issue of blood for twelve years, she suffered many things at the hands of many physicians, and she spent all that she had without getting better. In fact, she continually grew worse. Today, it is no different for many women. Almost daily, I see women with strikingly similar stories. When they suffer from female problems, they typically go to physicians, and in many cases, for an extended period of many years. These women suffer with many different ailments such as fatigue, irritability, hair loss, anxiety, sweats, cramping, depression, vaginal dryness, excess bleeding, etc. They waste all their hard-earned money on toxic synthetic treatments, yet their health does not improve and they continue to get sicker over time despite the fact that they are under a doctor's care.

The woman with the issue of blood was healed because of her faith. We could all learn a lesson from her example. She knew that if she just touched the hem of His garment, she would be healed. She was exactly right. We must seek Jesus for our healing, as He is Jehovah Rophe our healer, not any earthly physician. Regardless of whether a person is male or female, the one who suffers most is the person who trusts in physicians rather than exercising his or her faith in God. It is the Lord who created mankind and knows exactly what is needed for recovery.

My wife is five feet, three inches tall, one hundred and sixteen pounds and gorgeous! I married the woman of my dreams in 1982 and she has given me three beautiful children. She has no need of physicians, and there is not a woman I have seen that can hold a candle to her physical beauty, strength and endurance. She has taken Mark 5:25-26 as a warning and has stayed away from the world's system of medicine. We have prayed and followed the Lord's leading to achieve healing the way He intended, and for many years, we have walked side-by-side trusting our blessed Creator. We truly feel we are gaining health with age, and I think Amy's beauty today exceeds that of the day I met her.

A Better Way

Rejecting the entire "medication" approach and embracing the natural remedies available through God's abundant creation, sets you free to heal. Your body will often even heal faster without the interference of pharmakeia. For example, after having oral surgery, one of my clients Rachel, was told by her dentist that she had to take antibiotics as a precaution against infection. Since Rachel had been a client for some time, she knew the detrimental effects of antibiotics and how they weaken the immune system. She chose not to take them and instead used the following:

- Neem oil on her gums three times daily
- One teaspoon of buffered mineral ascorbate vitamin C three times daily
- A probiotic blend of ten strains of beneficial bacteria for mouth and intestinal balance
- Echinacea as an immune-supportive herbal remedy

At Rachel's follow up visit, her dentist commented on how rapidly she had healed and how healthy her gums looked. Rachel refused the antibiotic treatment, and by building up her body, she was restored to abundant health. Rachel chose the professional, quality nutritional products from our clinic rather than falling prey to deceptive advertising and marketing schemes that may have put her health at risk.

One of the greatest purposes for writing *The Trinity Diet* is best explained in Hosea 4:6 where it says, *"My people are destroyed for lack of knowledge. Because you have rejected knowledge, I also will reject you..."* I share this information with you so your health will not be destroyed. I pray you will not reject it. I get so excited when I imagine the victory you will have when applying these God-given principles. Jesus Christ is the deliverer of His people and can set you free from sickness and disease.

The Narrow Road that Leads to Life

The individuals who come to our Nutrition and Health Center and choose to change their lifestyles are usually very excited at first, but some find that the pressures of the world, family and friends become too numerous for them to continue on. For example, a woman named Mary came into our office experiencing severe hot flashes. She was taking an estrogen medication she didn't want to take. While she was fearful of the medication, she was also scared to stop taking it because she was told her bones would become brittle and break. Unfortunately, one of the ways sorcery gains control of our lives is through fear which pressures patients into taking medication. This is all too common in the United States as proven by the fact that Americans are the largest consumers of medication in the world.

When Mary decided to eliminate the medication and try natural plant hormone-supportive nutrients instead, she came under attack from family, friends and coworkers who projected their fear onto her and began to scare her into returning to the drugs and doctors. I'm sure they did this out of genuine concern for Mary, but that doesn't make it right. These friends and family were telling her to return to the doctor because they could not trust God to bring the healing that He promises in His Word when we follow His commands.

Many people perish for lack of knowledge in health and wellness. Thankfully, Mary was not one of them. She was convinced that God was leading her in a new direction and took a higher, more difficult road which offered a much greater reward of abundant health in this life and the life to come. Mary has stable strong bones and no fear of rejecting medication. She is free.

Jesus instructed us to *"enter through the narrow gate. For wide is the gate and broad is the road that leads to destruction, and many enter through it. But small is the gate and narrow the road that leads to life, and only a few find it"* (Matt. 7:13-14). *The Trinity Diet* may be a narrow road, but it is a road that leads to life for you and your family.

A New Thing

With great expectation, grab hold of the promise of health and healing the Lord has for you. You too are called to this promise of abundance in the body. The Lord desires you to live that promise more than you desire it for yourself; so pray and ask Him for help to find the way to health. Ask Him to wipe away your past choices of sin, death and destruction. In Isaiah 1:19, He says, *"If you are willing and obedient, you shall eat the good of the land."*

I was obedient to follow God as he drew me nearer to Him and away from the old life of prescription drugs, toxic foods and negative thoughts. You also are called to look no longer to the past. You are called into obedience to God, just as Christ was obedient in going to the cross. It is your turn to take up your cross, crucify your flesh, and look to the cross of Christ for freedom in your health. A clean body makes way for the mind to be clear and to think on Godly things. Offer your body as a living sacrifice before the Lord, and ask the Lord to help purify your spirit, soul and body.

CHAPTER 7

CLEANSING AND
DETOXIFICATION

"Cleanse me with hyssop, and I will be clean; wash me, and I will be whiter than snow."
PSALM 51:7

HOW MANY times recently have you heard of someone going through a cleansing or detoxification program? It seems as though this is the latest health craze, and everyone seems to be jumping on board. While there are many approaches that claim to support this natural process, "detoxification" is nothing more than a normal process your body performs throughout the day. *The Trinity Diet* focuses on providing an adequate balance of the nutrients your body needs to optimize its ongoing detoxification process.

In order to detoxify itself, the body removes toxic waste via the feces, urine, carbon dioxide, and sweat. Internally, organs such as the liver, kidney, lungs, gallbladder, and spleen are continually working to remove waste from the body. This is a vital function that combats the more than one hundred thousand bacterial microbes which invade our bodies every day. In the United States alone, we are subject to more than 2.4 billion pounds of chemical toxins in one year. Our bodies were simply not designed to remove toxins in such massive amounts. The continuous exposure to dietary and environmental toxins, may lead to an impaired ability to metabolize and clear damage-causing compounds from the body.

According to an October 2007 *Harper's Magazine* article on toxins in the blood, "The common American has an average of over

200 foreign toxic chemicals in their blood at any one time."[7] The Environmental Working Group reports, "Tap water in 42 states is contaminated with more than 140 unregulated chemicals."[8]

In addition, the Environmental Protection Agency (EPA) conducted an adipose tissue survey of more than thirty-three thousand U.S. residents and found styrene, dichlorobenzene, xylene, and ethylphenol in 100 percent of the tissue samples. These toxic chemicals have dangerous, detrimental effects on human health.[9]

This was a particularly relevant survey, because the adipose tissue is fat that accumulates in the body and around the midsection. The body uses adipose tissue as a means to safely deposit toxins away from critical organs and the blood. This process protects the body until it is able to remove the toxic substances through its natural detoxification process. Unfortunately, most people do not eat or supplement in a way that supports detoxification; consequently their bodies age, continuing to become fatter and more toxic. Below is a list of symptoms associated with the accumulation of toxins in the body.

- General malaise
- Fatigue
- Headaches
- Joint pain
- Muscle pain
- Chronic mucus production
- Poor exercise tolerance
- Skin rashes
- Edema
- Immune weakness
- Environmental and chemical sensitivities
- Mental status changes (inability to concentrate, depression, mood changes, memory loss, sleep disturbances, anxiety, etc.)

[7] Schapiro, M. (2007, October). Toxic inaction: Why poisonous, unregulated chemicals end up in our blood. *Harper's Magazine*. Retrieved December 14, 2009 from, http://harpers.org/archive/2007/10/0081742.

[8] Environmental Working Group. (n.d.). *Unregulated Contaminants*. Retrieved December 14, 2009, from http://www.ewg.org/node/28272?file=unregcontams.

[9] Patient Education: Role of Detoxification in Chronic Disease. (n.d.). Retrieved December 14, 2009, from http://74.125.95.132/search?q=cache:TNBTbfLqRRYJ:future ofmedicine.

The Importance of Hydration

One of the most effective ways to combat and flush toxins from the body is to drink an adequate amount of purified water throughout the day. This amazing chemical combination of hydrogen and oxygen, known as H O, is yet another reflection of the triune nature of God and is referenced 396 times in the Bible. Its trinity formation includes liquid, vapor (steam) and solid (ice). According to research data, water is the most important element in the detoxification process, yet 75 percent of Americans are chronically dehydrated. In one study, just a 2 percent drop in water was shown to trigger fuzzy, short-term memory, trouble with basic math, and a reduced ability to focus. It is not surprising then, that a lack of water is the number one trigger of daytime fatigue. Mild dehydration has also been shown to slow down metabolism.

The benefits of water are just as significant! Drinking only five glasses of water per day has been shown to decrease the risk of colon cancer by 45 percent and breast cancer by 79 percent. Another study found that eight to ten glasses of water per day could significantly ease back and joint pain in 80 percent of sufferers. While a study conducted by the University of Washington, found that one glass of water would shut down midnight hunger pangs in almost 100 percent of the dieters studied. As you can see, being well hydrated is vital to our health, yet a majority of the "wise" physicians of this world's system, never take time to assess whether a person is dehydrated. In I Corinthians 1:27, the word says, "... *God deliberately chose things the world considers foolish in order to shame those who think they are wise. And he chose those who are powerless to shame those who are powerful.*" Assessing hydration is such a simple test, yet many deem it as foolish. In my practice, 90 percent of the people that come into my office for their first visit are dehydrated. We immediately increase their consumption of water, and within hours, we see a miraculous improvement in their body chemistry.

The simple step of drinking an adequate amount of water can make a significant difference in your body. One of our clients, a youth pastor named Patrick, was motivated to eliminate sodas from his diet after he attended a nutrition class Amy and I presented at his church. He replaced his usual soda intake with two gallons of water every day, and in two months, this six-foot-tall young man went from weighing 265 pounds to 230 pounds. He didn't change anything else in his diet or lifestyle and lost 35 pounds. This is quite a remarkable biological transformation of the body, that resulted from an intake of water, and the elimination of one of America's favorite toxic drinks—sodas.

Water is also critical to the liver's ability to remove chemicals that have broken down to a water-soluble state in order to be taken out through the kidneys during the body's natural detoxification process. Just as water is vital for your washing machine to really clean your clothes, the liver needs water to really clean the toxins from your body. If you were to eliminate most of the water needed to clean your clothes, you would be disappointed with the results. The clothes would not come out as clean, and over time, the colors would become dull. In the same way, what if you could only use one to two cups of water for your shower or bath? That amount of water would not be sufficient to achieve a clean body on the outside. Obviously, it requires a much larger amount of water to wash the outside of your body. This is vitally true for the inside of your body as well. Your body must have water in order to remove toxins that are broken down by the liver which will later be excreted from the kidneys. At a cellular level, water is required to transport nutrition into the cells for energy production and toxins out of the cells to be excreted from the body.

Many times when a person is toxic, they will notice swelling in their hands and feet, or even in the abdomen. The body does this as a defense mechanism to dilute toxins and store them in the extra-cellular water compartments of the body. Later, when the body has the necessary nutrients and water to convert the toxins, it will remove the toxins and reduce the swelling. Ironically, many individuals with swelling are afraid to drink water. They think it will cause them to swell more, but it is actually the lack of water that is causing the swelling. Sandra came to our office with kidney failure and on dialysis. She had been told not to drink too much water, when what she really needed was to increase her water intake. Her kidneys needed water to filter out toxins; instead, she was on twelve medications that were poisoning her body. We had her drink two to three quarts of water a day along with other restorative nutrients, and soon she was doing much better. However, this was an uphill battle. Doctors had strongly advised her not to drink too much water. She had been told by them to take prescription drugs and to make preparations for death. Instead, ten years later, she has a degree in Education, is happily married and is living in Virginia.

Water for Cleansing

Cleansing may appear to be a growing fad among those seeking better health, but it is as ancient as Old Testament times. An excerpt from the *Dead Sea Scrolls* written fifteen hundred years before the birth of Jesus Christ gave the following instructions:

> Seek, therefore, a large trailing gourd, having a stalk the length of a man; take out its inwards and fill it with water from the river which the sun has warmed. Hang it upon the branch of a tree, and kneel upon the ground before the angel of water, and suffer the end of the stalk of the trailing gourd to enter your hinder parts, that the water may flow through all your bowels, then, let the water run out from your body, that it may carry away from within it all the unclean and evil- smelling things of Satan. And you shall see with your eyes and smell with your nose all the abominations and uncleanness which defiled the temple of your body. Even all the sins, which abode in your body, tormenting you with all manner of pains. Renew your baptizing with water on every day of your fast, till the day when you see that the water which flows out of you is as pure as the river's foam.[10]

After reading this passage for the first time, I realized how much more our bodies need cleansing today, than they even did in the past. They didn't have our toxic food, toxic environment, or stress and still they found it essential for maintaining health in the body, soul and spirit. Today, the ancient trailing gourd has been replaced with a modern process we call colon hydrotherapy that gently and safely irrigates the colon. In our clinic, patients who participate in our colon cleansing programs experience a number of health benefits, including reduced headaches, better bowel elimination, healthier skin, and clearer thinking. It is a regular part of our family's health regiment, and I recommend it for all those who come to our office.

Colon hydrotherapy is performed in our clinic with an FDA- certified system that provides a dignified and hygienic way to cleanse the colon to the same degree as twenty enemas—which is why it was once called a "high enema." Many naturopathic professionals today recommend colon irrigation for all types of conditions, and it can be performed before any

---

[10] Curtis, B. (1993). Remove the Thorn & God Will Heal. Victorville, CA: Bud Curtis.

endoscopic procedures, as a substitute for drinking chemical laxatives. You can find out more about this amazing procedure, as well as locations that offer this service in your area at www.angelofwater.com. Included on the website is a brief animation that will give you a better understanding of this process.

Toxin Overload

Toxins are found in every corner of the earth and are absorbed through the skin, mouth, lungs, and digestive tract daily. Even as our bodies work overtime to try to remove these toxins, many of us are losing the battle as evidenced by the rise of chronic degenerative disease in our country. While we can't escape many of these toxins, we can take supportive nutrients and herbs that assist the body with detoxification.

We can also follow the principles set forth in this book.

One area that is often overlooked is our skin. It is the largest organ of the body, and it plays a significant role in the detoxification process. What we eat not only affects our internal organs, but this external organ as well. Our food choices are as important for the skin as they are for any other organ. In addition, the skin is highly permeable, and General malaise what we put on our skins have direct access to our bloodstream. It is important to carefully evaluate the products we choose for skin and body care needs.

A good rule of thumb is to only put on your skin what you would be willing to eat. This isn't always easy. Research shows that the average consumer has only a 2.5-percent chance of selecting a nutritional, non-toxic, and effective product off the shelf. This was confirmed in a landmark study reported in the *Journal of the American Nutraceutical Association* in winter of 1999. While toxic ingredients in skin and body care products are now commonplace, we can learn to read labels and avoid chemicals that can interfere with healthy organ function, create hormonal imbalance, and mutate healthy cells into unhealthy ones. Avoid products that contain any of the following ingredients:

Propylene glycol	Mineral oil
Sodium lauryl sulfate (SLS)	Parabens (propyl, methyl, butyl, ethyl)
Synthetic colors	Imidazolidinyl and diazolidinyl urea
Fragrance	Triethanoliamine (TEA)

Internally, be sure your diet includes key nutrients for radiant skin, such as vitamin C, zinc, fish oils, vitamin D3, Vitamin E, probiotics, and of course, a balance of your *Trinity Diet* macro nutrients. Another effective tool for skin detoxification is the infra-red sauna, which removes seven times more toxins in sweat than regular sweating caused from other sources. It is also beneficial for weight loss, reducing blood pressure and cholesterol, pain relief, fine lines and wrinkles, and better circulation. We recommend it to all our clients at our clinic.

Since there are so many environmental factors we can't control, we need to be that much more diligent to do the things we can, in order to realize our own testimonies of God's healing power in our lives. In I Corinthians 3:16-17, we are challenged, *"Do you not know that you are a temple of God and {that} the Spirit of God dwells in you? If any man destroys the temple of God, God will destroy him, for the temple of God is holy, and that is what you are."*

We can't change the past. If we have made poor food, skin and body care choices— which most of us have, we can repent and begin to make better choices today. I believe God will help us. Psalm 37:5 encourages us, *"Commit to the Lord whatever you do and your plans will succeed."*

Let's work together to help restore, rebuild, and transform God's people into living temples testifying to His mighty healing power. As Romans 12:1-2 instructs us, we need to *"give {our} bodies to God."* Let them be a living and holy sacrifice—the kind He will accept. When you think of what He has done for you, is this too much to ask? Don't copy the behavior and customs of this world, but let God transform you into a new person by changing the way you think. Then you will know what God wants you to do and you will know how *"good and pleasing and perfect"* His will really is.

Ask the Lord to help you build up your body so you may fulfill your calling in this life with abundant living.

Water to Wash and Refresh

Psalm 1:3 (KJV) describes what we can expect when we walk in the ways of the Lord. It says, *"And he shall be like a tree planted by the rivers of water, that brings forth his fruit in his season; his leaf also shall not wither; and whatsoever he does shall prosper."* A tree that is planted by rivers of water is able to bear much fruit and will not wither or fade. I believe this scripture can represent our physical and emotional well being as well. The body and the blood require an abundant water supply in order to bear the fruit of physical effort. We must drink an abundance of water for our bodies to function according to their divine design. Just as a tree planted by a river of water will bear much fruit, when we drink an adequate amount of water, we too will bear much fruit. A good rule of thumb is to drink a minimum of one-half your body weight in ounces of water per day for optimal support of detoxification and hydration of the cells. When exercising or working outside in the heat, you need to drink an additional eight to sixteen ounces of water for every hour of labor.

Herbal and Nutritional Support for Detoxification

The liver requires a wide range of nutrients to help the body convert fat-soluble toxins to a more water-soluble form so that they can be more easily removed from the body through urine, sweat, and waste. Water alone will help, but your *Trinity Diet* should be fortified with many of the herbal remedies that God put on the planet for this very reason. Even after Adam and Eve were removed from the perfect living conditions in the Garden of Eden and the Lord cursed the ground, He still caused milk thistle to grow. Not surprisingly, milk thistle is one of many herbal remedies that supports the detoxification and protection of the liver. Even when we go astray and the Lord disciplines us, He is merciful. At the same time that He cursed the earth because of our sin, He yet showed His love for us, by providing a number of herbal supports for our bodies.

Let's go back to our example of how the liver uses water to remove toxins, just as a washing machine removes dirt from clothing. To take this analogy a step further, after placing clothes in the washer, soap is then added to assist the cleansing process.

Without soap, water alone will not do an adequate job of removing the dirt from the clothes. It is the same with the liver. Water alone cannot remove all of the toxins from the body. Adequate nutritional support is required to break down the toxins to a more water-soluble condition. This support is available in specially blended detoxification formulas that are designed to assist the body in removing environmental toxins. They combine nutrients in balanced quantities to effectively support this procedure. These nutritional formulas can be purchased from our clinic or from many health care clinics that support natural health. Chiropractic doctors, certified clinical nutritionists, naturopathic doctors, a few medical doctors and doctors of osteopathic medicine, carry these products as well. My favorite detoxification products are Ultra Clear Plus, Lipo Gen, Adva Clear, SP Cleanse, and DetoxN Guard. Many of their ingredients are discussed in the next chapter of easy herbal remedies.

In the fall of 2005, we received a call from a dedicated client named Cathy who had wandered off the trail of health and found herself in the emergency room with abdominal pain. Cathy had been a client for less than a year and was still experimenting with medications to deal with various pains and problems. After being rushed to the emergency room, medical specialists told Cathy that the problem was her gallbladder, and that it had to be removed. After hearing this, Cathy remembered a time when we had helped her cleanse her gallbladder. She told the doctor she wanted to keep her gallbladder and promptly left the hospital. She arrived at our office a few hours later to cleanse her gallbladder. We spent an hour together using nutrients such as magnesium, olive oil, and some bitter herbs to begin the process of dissolving toxins and cleansing her gallbladder and other organs. She felt a bit of nausea for a couple of days, but within three days, she was fine. She has continued her recommended health program, and many years later, she is living an abundant life with her gallbladder in place.

Cleansing in the Wilderness

When Moses led the Israelites out of captivity in Egypt and into the wilderness, he was followed by nearly three million men, women, and children. Exodus 15:22-27 tells of a time when there was no water to be found, but the Lord provided:

> So Moses brought Israel from the Red Sea; then they went out into the Wilderness of Shur. And they went three days in the wilderness and found no water. Now when they came to Marah, they could not drink the waters of Marah, for they were bitter. Therefore, the name of it was

called Marah, and the people complained against Moses, saying, "What shall we drink?" So he cried out to the Lord, and the Lord showed him a tree. When he cast it into the waters, the waters were made sweet. There he made a statute and an ordinance for them, and there he tested them, and said, "If you diligently heed the voice of the Lord your God and do what is right in his sight, give ear to his commandments and keep all his statutes, I will put none of the diseases on you which I have brought on the Egyptians. For I am the Lord who heals you." Then they came to Elim, where there were twelve wells of water and seventy palm trees; so they camped there by the waters.

On the surface, this appears to be a story of God quenching the Israelites' thirst. But I believe it is a story of God's provision for cleansing their polluted bodies from the poor lifestyle and dietary habits of the Egyptians. I believe the plan was to drink the bitter waters of Marah to initiate a flush of their internal organs, such as the kidney, liver, intestines, spleen, heart, and circulation. Here's why. The waters of Marah have been tested and found to have high levels of magnesium. Magnesium salt is what makes the water bitter and appear milky. There are many benefits of magnesium, which include improved muscle function, heart health, and nerve function. It also helps break up toxic fatty and calcified buildup to support better liver, gallbladder, and colon elimination of toxic waste. Instead of being obedient and drinking the waters of Marah to initiate a flush, the Israelites grumbled and didn't trust the Lord's instruction. So, the Lord told Moses to break off a branch from a tree nearby, and throw it into the water to make it sweet. Even today, there remains a certain tree that grows in the region around the waters of Marah, whose sap when placed into its' waters, causes the magnesium salt to sink leaving the top clear and sweet to drink.

In Exodus 15:26, the Lord declares that His healing is conditional for His people. It requires obedience to His word and His ways. This passage demonstrates that God is faithful and full of mercy even when we disobey. However, we can miss out on the blessings that would be ours if we would just obey. When the Israelites approached Marah, although they were desperate for water, they refused the water God led them to. Despite this, the Lord still provided making the waters sweet and by later leading them to a place of paradise with fresh spring water and seventy palm trees. Sadly, I still believe they missed out on what God had for them at Marah. They did not understand that the Lord wanted to cleanse them physically to give their minds and bodies healthier function to endure the temptations and testing that the wilderness would bring. They, like us, were impatient and needed to trust the Lord's timing for health and healing. The Israelites received the abundance of water, but missed the benefits of having their bodies cleansed by the magnesium salt.

Daily Cleansing Habits

Here is a simple process you can follow on a daily basis to safely cleanse your body.

1. Drink half your body weight in ounces of water per day to assist with the removal of toxins.
2. Eat clean foods from the allowed list provided in the Detoxification Shopping List that follows.
3. Consider a medical food and herbs to assist with the detoxification of your organs and whole body.
4. Eliminate foods and processed foods that contribute to toxins in the body.
5. Consider colon irrigation to assist the body's removal of waste.

Below are a number of testimonies from people who followed these five simple steps with significant results:

*   Sandy lowered her cholesterol from 289 to 190 in three weeks.
*   Jill lost fifteen pounds of fluid in three days.
*   Rebecca reduced her liver enzymes (liver burden) to qualify for her life insurance exam.
*   Nancy, age seventy, had been waiting for ten years to have a liver transplant because of a hepatitis C diagnosis. Her doctor removed her from that list when her liver markers returned to normal after six weeks on a detoxification program.
*   Bill lowered his systolic and diastolic blood pressure each thirty-five points in three months.
*   Joyce has not had a headache for more than one year after having three migraines per week prior to detoxification.

- Robert lost seventy-five pounds and eliminated four medications.
- Mike has no more eczema.
- Sandra discontinued dialysis and ten medications after being told she had only six months to live.
- Stephen has no more anxiety attacks and angina pain in his heart.

We pray that you, too, will have a testimony that will break the power of the enemy in your life, as well as in the lives of others you will impact for Christ.

Detoxification Shopping List

This shopping list provides helpful guidelines for food selections that will aid your body in daily detoxification. The purpose of a detoxification diet is to remove the most common immune-reactive foods. It is designed for individuals desiring to detoxify and reduce their risk of digestive intolerance to highly allergenic foods. We recommend that a person use these guidelines for twenty-one days during a metabolic detoxification program, and then re-introduce foods checking for sensitivities by following the food reintroduction guidelines provided at the end of this chapter.

During detoxification, we also recommended taking nutritional support such as Ultra Clear Plus, Lipo Gen, Adva Clear, SP Cleanse, and DetoxN Guard with professional guidance to assist you in a successful detoxification process. Maintenance support is then recommended to keep the body clean and operating most efficiently.

Meat, fish, poultry: Chicken, turkey, lamb, cold-water fish, such as salmon, halibut, and mackerel (look for wild caught fish with scales and fins)
Meat to avoid: Red meat, cold cuts, frankfurter, sausage, canned meats, eggs, pork, and any scavenger animals

Dairy products: Unsweetened live-culture yogurt, substitutes, such as rice milk, nut milks, and non-GMO soy beverages
Dairy products to avoid: Milk, cheese, ice cream, cream, non- dairy creamers, and cottage cheese

Starches: Yukon gold or sweet potatoes, rice, tapioca, buckwheat, and gluten-free products
Starches to avoid: All gluten-containing products, such as wheat, barley, spelt, oats, and corn.

Soups: Clear, vegetable-based broths, and homemade vegetarian soups
Soups to avoid: Canned or creamed soups

Vegetables: All vegetables, preferably fresh or frozen, legumes, dried peas, and lentils
Vegetables to avoid: Canned and creamed vegetables of any kind (including in casseroles)

Beverages: Unsweetened fruit or vegetable juices, water, non- citrus and caffeine-free herbal teas
Beverages to avoid: Milk, coffee, tea, cocoa, alcohol, sodas, sweetened beverages, and citrus drinks

Bread/cereals: Any made from rice, buckwheat, millet, soy, potato flour, tapioca, amaranth, quinoa, arrowroot, kamut, or gluten- free flour-based products
Bread/cereals to avoid: Gluten products, wheat, corn, oat, spelt, rye, and barley

Fruits: Fresh, frozen unsweetened, or water-packed apples, applesauce, apricots, bananas, blackberries, blueberries, cherries, kiwi, melons, papaya, pears, peaches, pineapple, plums, raspberries, and strawberries
Fruits to avoid: Oranges, fruit drinks, citrus fruits, and canned fruits (excluding citrus-dried fruit)

Fats/oils/nuts: Cold/expeller-pressed, unrefined canola, flax seed, and olive oils; sesame seeds, almonds, pecans, sunflower seeds, pumpkin seeds, pecans, walnuts, and squash seed/butters
Fats/oils/nuts to avoid: Margarine, shortening, unclarified butter, refined salad dressings and oils, peanuts and pistachios

Food Sensitivity Testing

If you suspect food allergies or want to check for food sensitivities, follow the steps below. These are the same steps you will follow to reintroduce foods to the diet.

1. Remove all food allergens most common to American diets, such as wheat, oats, gluten, milk, dairy products, corn, citrus, oranges, peanuts, pistachios, beef, and hydrogenated oils. Studies have shown these foods to be inflammatory, sensitizing, and immunosuppressive in a large majority of individuals.
2. Perform a detoxification program for twenty-one days to assist the body's natural process of clearing inflammatory toxins and food allergens from the body.
3. Re-introduce foods after twenty-one days using one food at a time in three-day intervals. This will provide some knowledge as to the sensitivity of your body to these foods.
4. Before eating any food you wish to test, take a pulse reading for three minutes while sitting down and relaxing.
5. Eat the desired food at a meal.
6. Wait fifteen minutes after the meal and retest the pulse.
7. If the pulse rises eight to ten points or more, you probably have sensitivity to that food.
8. Look for other delayed symptoms, such as headache, runny eyes, itching ears, brain fog, skin rash, and many other symptoms. These may experience within the next twenty-four hours as a result of the food sensitivity.
9. Repeat the test after three days on the next food to be tested.
10. If symptoms arise, limit the food to every four days or not at all depending on the severity of the symptoms. Please discuss this test with your health practitioner.

Use this chart to keep a record of the foods you try and your body's response.

FOOD	DATE AND TIME	REACTIONS

CHAPTER 8

EASY HERBAL
REMEDIES

"And God said, 'See, I have given you every herb that yields seed which is on the face of all the earth, and every tree whose fruit yields seed; to you it shall be for food."
GENESIS 1:29 (NLT)

WHEN GOD created the heavens and earth, He created herbs even before He created man. This was the third day of creation. I believe the Lord did this prior to man's inhabitation of the earth so as to prepare nutrient rich herbs and plants for our consumption. After creating man, God instructed Adam and Eve in Genesis 1:26, to go forth and multiply. Following that, He gave them specific instructions to eat of the herbs and partake of the fruits from the trees, saying, "... *they will be yours for food.*"

Herbs for Everyday Consumption

The miracle of plants is summed up in Revelation 22:2, which says, "... *the leaves of the tree were for the healing of the nations.*" Since the beginning of recorded history, plants have been the main source of medicine for people all over the world. So what exactly is an herb? An herb is a plant valued for its medicinal properties, flavor, scent, or the like. It may include the bark, flower, fruit, leaf, stem, or root of a plant. The vast and continuous science of using plants for healing is called herbology.

The earth's environment has changed enormously since creation, and our need for herbs is even more important today. Hippocrates, considered the father of medicine, said, "Let your food be your medicine and let your medicine be your food." Hippocrates stated a very important truth—there is no distinction between food and medicine. Food was, and is our medicine. Yet in this pharmaceutical age, many people have been fooled into believing food and medicine are two completely different things; that food is evil and medicine is good. Nothing could be further from the truth.

In this chapter, I have included a summary of my favorite herbal remedies and how they have been used historically in the body. Herbs can be used individually or in blended formulas for greater effectiveness. Personally, I consume more than twenty-five different herbs daily to support the ongoing challenge of keeping my body functioning optimally.

It is important to know that if you are taking prescription medication while consuming herbs, the side effects of these medications might be intensified. The herbs will nourish your cells and enhance cellular function, producing more aggressive removal of toxic substances from the body and making your pain receptors more sensitive. With healthier cellular function gained from taking herbs, medications will often become more efficient. The side effects from medications may also increase as a result.

Following is a list of health conditions and herbs used to support the physiological needs of the body. These are the herbs we use most often with our clients at the Nutrition and Health Center and in our family.

Pain and Inflammation Support

Herbs are an excellent means for addressing pain and inflammation. At age twenty-nine, Francesca was diagnosed with severe rheumatoid arthritis. Most days, she was unable to walk or even move from the couch. After one year of following *The Trinity Diet*, detoxifying, and using a natural anti-inflammation support program, she became free of both pain and medications. The year after that, she had her second child, and now three years later, she is still arthritis free. Many of the herbs listed below were a part of the personal nutrition program we developed for her at our health center.

- Frankincense, or boswellia, has been used in traditional herbal medicine for chronic inflammation. The organic acids in boswellia inhibit an enzyme involved in inflammation synthesis.

- Curcumin from the turmeric plant is the yellow pigment from the plant. Curcuma longa has been used traditionally to treat sprains and inflammation. While pain medications typically produce significant toxicity, curcumin does not. The very low incidence of dementia or Alzheimer's in males over age sixty-five in India is attributed to the high intake of curcumin in the diet.
- Bromelain has been helpful in reducing inflammation in cases of joint disease, sports injury, or trauma, and it prevents swelling after trauma or surgery.
- White willow bark is another herb that traditionally has been used to treat pain. It contains salicin, which is the precursor to salicylic acid, and it works as an anti-fever and anti-pain agent. By taking willow bark, the salicin is converted to salicylic acid in the blood stream. This is an alternative to taking salicylic acid in the form of aspirin, which is known to cause intestinal damage and bleeding.
- Ginger is an excellent herb that has anti-inflammatory properties. It inhibits platelet aggregation in which the blood becomes too sticky for proper circulation. Ginger is excellent as a hot tea and can be purchased dehydrated for use in many foods, juices and smoothies.
- Quercetin is a yellow-green favonoid from the sacred Saphora japonica tree that, in its soluble, monomeric, low-molecular-weight form helps reduce allergic and inflammatory responses, by promoting repair of the delicate cell membranes. Research also has confirmed quercetin's anti-viral and antioxidant benefits.

Immune System Support

Echinacea angustifolia and echinacea purpurea are two powerful herbs that assist the body's natural defenses and enhance the immune system's ability to repair and communicate. Each has properties that are unique, and the blending of angustifolia and purpurea will:

- Enhance non-specific immune system support;
- Support and maintain healthy throat tissue;
- Help the immune system produce protein-like molecules called interferon, which are released by white blood cells (lymphocytes) to respond to the presence of foreign invaders, such as viruses, bacteria, parasites, or tumor cells;

- Support and promote healthy white blood cells;
- Support healthy immune response following stress and sudden climate changes;
- Enhance upper respiratory function;
- Support healthy lymphatic system function; and,
- Stimulate the body's normal tissue support and renewal function.

This combination of herbs was used by natives to treat spider bites and snake bites. It was also used by our son, Jason, when he received a severe spider bite while attending college in Dallas. Out of fear, friends insisted that he go to the hospital. He immediately called me to ask for advice. I told him to go to the health food store and purchase the most expensive echinacea formula available. He took five capsules three times a day, along with high doses of a fully reduced ascorbate form of vitamin C, to induce a bowel flush and support lymphocyte activity. A week later, he returned home with friends for spring break. The bite on his arm had swollen and was full of white blood cells (otherwise known as pus). We increased his immune-building nutrients and water intake, while heating his arm with a hot washcloth. Finally, we lanced the bump and squeezed the area to drive the pus out of his arm. A large amount of pus, blood, and dark toxic matter was removed from his arm. The sore dried up and healed a week later. He was patient to wait on the Lord's healing and received it without an emergency room visit and without medication.

Cardiovascular and Circulation Support

Hawthorn and garlic are two herbs that are known to promote cardiovascular and circulatory health. Hawthorn contains many phytonutrients that support cardiovascular system. The plant leaf has a unique shape similar to the human heart, and the berries are bright red. Interestingly, the stems of the berries resemble the shape of human capillaries.

Hawthorn supports normal functioning of the heart muscle, normal blood pressure within a normal range, normal coronary blood flow, cardiovascular system health, and provides antioxidant protection.

Garlic is also excellent for cardiovascular and circulatory health. Garlic is known to have more properties for health benefits than the majority of known herbs and plants. We use this every day, pressing fresh garlic on everything from fish and chicken to steamed veggies. We also use it in our salad dressing. Garlic is an amazing substance that:

- Helps maintain normal cholesterol levels within a normal range
- Supports cardiovascular health
- Promotes anti-platelet activity
- Encourages a healthy intestinal environment to help maintain proper gastrointestinal flora
- Enhances immune system response
- Promotes healthy lung function.

Detoxification and Digestive Support

The combination of globe artichoke, milk thistle and fringe tree, provides key phytochemicals to assist with the natural process of detoxification. These herbs and the many compounds within them combine to:

- Promote feelings of renewed vitality, energy, and well-being by supporting multifunctional detoxification
- Enhance the actions of several liver detoxification enzymes while promoting balanced activity of the detoxification pathways
- Support healthy liver and gallbladder function
- Support the normal processing of hormones in the body
- Encourage healthy digestive function
- Enhance healthy bowel function
- Encourage the healthy function of the organs for elimination
- Help maintain healthy blood through natural purification

These three herbs also possess the ability to balance cholesterol by removing excess bad cholesterol (LDL) and increasing good cholesterol (HDL).

Stress, Mood, and Energy Support

Stress is an epidemic problem in America today and most physicians are not addressing the issue to help people overcome its negative effects on the body. Every individual who comes to our center receives some type of herbal support for stress. Many of these herbs, called adaptogens, are designed to help the body adapt to stress. With the demands placed on our bodies because of our hectic lifestyles, stress deeply influences mood, mental function, and the cognitive process. The ongoing effects of stress cause multiple systemic problems throughout the body effecting organs such as the heart, the liver, the kidneys, thyroid, adrenals, brain, and digestive tract.

Signs of low adrenal function due to excess stress include an uncontrollable appetite, mood swings, lack of recuperative sleep, increased pain and inflammation, lack of proper blood sugar control, decreased immune function, and abdominal weight gain. As a result of stress and fatigue, people often push themselves to continue functioning, many times with the help of stimulants. Eventually, this leads to debility and severe fatigue as the energy producing hormones are diminished without adequate nutritional support.

The twelve herbs listed below are used synergistically in a formula we recommend for dealing with stress and the related health problems. These herbs work better together and should be purchased in a combined formula instead of buying the herbs individually. You can purchase this combination in a product called Serenegen by Metagenics. It is known to help maintain equilibrium between body systems and promote a sense of inner calm. It also provides herbal support for those who have difficulty resting, are over-worked, sleep-deprived, and/or depleted of physical reserves. It can be taken in the evening and during the day as needed for anxiety, nervousness and tension. Here are the herbs that are included in the combination:

- Rehmannia root (rehmannia glutinosa)
- Schisandra fruit (schisandra chinensis)
- Jujube fruit (zizyphus spinosa)
- Dong quai root (angelica sinensis)
- Chinese asparagus root (asparagus cochinchinensis)
- Ophiopogon root (ophiopogon japonicus)
- Scrophularia root (scrophularia ningpoensis)
- Asian ginseng root (panax ginseng)
- Chinese salvia root (salvia miltiorrhiza)

- Poria fungus (wolfporia cocos)
- Polygala root (polygala tenuifolia)
- Platycodon root (platycodon grandiforum)

Rhodiola is another popular plant used in Eastern Europe and Asia to address stress and its related symptoms. It is now becoming quite common in the United States as more people become aware of its ability to balance the central nervous system, decrease depression, enhance work performance and endurance, eliminate fatigue, stabilize and regulate moods, and protect cardio functions. Research has also found that rhodiola can help restore healthy sleep rhythms and improve poor appetite, irritability, hypertension, and mysterious headaches.

There are also two Asian trees that are known to help with stress. The magnolia officinalis is a tree native to the rain forests of China. Its bark has long been used in a variety of ways, including stress and anxiety control. The phellodendron, or the amur corktree grows in north-eastern China, and Japan. It has also been used throughout history for stress- related issues. Rhodiola, magnolia and phellodendron extracts are used in one of our stress formulas called Adreno Distress Guard by Perque, to support or restore levels of the cortisol and DHEA hormones in the body. This formula can be found at our clinic or may be ordered from our website at: www.nutritionandhealthcenter.com

Blood Sugar Support

The problem of blood sugar imbalance is a serious issue in America today. The majority of Americans ingest too many carbohydrates and struggle with consuming the right balance of foods. This is creating an ever increasing problem that will not be resolved until people are willing to follow the Lord by eating His live foods. In addition to eating a nutritional balance of foods as outlined in *The Trinity Diet*, taking any of the following ancient herbal remedies will also support glucose balance and energy in the cell.

- French lilac has been known since the Middle Ages to relieve the symptoms of diabetes mellitus. The active ingredient in this plant is known to lower blood sugar by decreasing insulin resistance. Chemical derivatives from this plant were approved by the FDA in 1995 for use by drug manufactures for medications to treat diabetes.

- Bitter melon is a plant related to the Chinese cucumber. It is commonly consumed as a vegetable in Asia and has long been used as an adjunct in diabetes management. Additionally, it has anti-bacterial and anti-parasitic properties. Bitter melon also has the potential to down- regulate insulin and is thought to slow down the aging process.
- Huckleberry/bilberry has been used traditionally in the treatment of diabetes. Research suggests that its leaf extract can lower blood sugar levels.
- Gymnema and fenugreek work to uphold healthy blood sugar levels. When combined with a *Trinity Diet*, they also preserve normal cholesterol levels in a healthy range, and support healthy blood lipid levels, including triglycerides.

Female Hormone Support

Chaste tree berry contains flavonoids and other compounds which together promote a natural, healthy balance of progesterone for female endocrine system balance. Chaste tree supports the activation of the endocrine glands to facilitate optimal progesterone production. This formula is ideal for women who still have ovarian function. It has been used for centuries, back to the time of Hippocrates, for female complaints associated with pre-menstrual syndrome (PMS) and painful menstruation. Chaste tree also supports healthy menstrual cycles, eases discomfort associated with PMS, enables normal reproductive function and progesterone balance, preserves healthy skin where hormone imbalance is suspect in both women and men, and eases tension associated with the menstrual cycle.

Post Menopause Support

Black cohosh is an herb traditionally used by women during menopause for relief of menopausal symptoms such as hot flashes and night sweats, irritability, mood swings, and sleep disturbances. Lemon balm and motherwort are adjunctive supporting herbs traditionally used to ease tension and support relaxation.

Depression, Anxiety and Nervous Tension Support

St John's wort is used in Europe to treat 90 percent of all cases of depression. It has also been used for sciatica and other nerve inflammation problems. I personally experienced sciatic nerve pain sporadically for more than twenty-four years. Since my daily intake of St. John's Wort, I have not had a sciatic fare up in the last eight years. Additional herbs such as valerian, jujube fruit, hops, passion flower, kava and rehmannia have beneficial effects on the nervous system as well.

Male Reproductive Support

For men, saw palmetto, nettle root, and pumpkin seed are known to support healthy urinary tract and prostate gland function. These herbs also support healthy bladder tissue and function, and ease smooth muscle spasms.

Using Herbs Effectively

In this chapter, we have covered the majority of the body's systems and their supportive herbs. Herbal remedies are available for just about any ailment today, but you have to be careful to choose quality products in order to avoid pesticide and chemical residues that can cause more health problems. Professional pharmaceutical-grade products are available through many natural health care providers.

When taking herbs, you will want to test your body for functional needs on a regular basis in order to determine your specific needs. This can be done by testing your saliva hormones, blood, and urine. Functional health need testing can be done through our clinic or any other comparative natural health care organization.

We encourage you to take this information and make herbs a part of your *Trinity Diet* to enable you to live the abundant life you were called to live.

CHAPTER 9

THE TRINITY OF
FITNESS

"For bodily exercise is profitable..."
I TIMOTHY 4:8 (ASV)

IN ORDER to bring balance to the body, soul and spirit, we must incorporate fitness or exercise into our lifestyle. The trinity of fitness includes aerobic (cardiovascular), strength, and flexibility training. Good physical health gives us the bodily strength and vitality to accomplish what God put us on earth to do—bring glory to His name.

My zeal for exercise began at age fourteen. I had always loved to run and play with friends, riding our bikes all over town. However, it was my traumatic eighth grade run-in with Jim Jenkins that changed my perspective of exercise forever. Jim and I sat at the same table in art class, and when I turned around before class to talk to him one day, he placed his hand on the bare part of my left arm and said to me, "Boy, you have weenie arms!" I was mortified! All I could do was turn around, speechless. I was a wimp, and the sting of his words drove me to do something about it. Let's face it men, we hate to be called wimps, and weenie arms just won't do. So the next week, I signed up for an extra-credit weight lifting class that was held after school. I was not going to be called a weenie ever again. Within a few months, there was a huge difference in my appearance. One day in weight lifting class, Jim's girlfriend was there and I don't think he appreciated how she looked at me. Jim Jenkins never called me a wimp again.

Exercise has always been, a part of our family's lifestyle. Even when we go on vacation, we always plan for physical activity because it is something all of us love to do. One summer, we traveled to Colorado and spent hours hiking in the beautiful Rocky Mountains. This activity enabled us to incorporate all three components of fitness into our exercise time. Our son, Jason, commented before the hike that it would probably not be a challenge for him. Much to his surprise however, the trail ascended 1,000 feet in just a couple of miles. Although Jason was indeed the first to reach the peak, he realized it was a pretty tough workout after all! As our family gathered at the top of the trail, we marveled at and were blessed by the wonders of God's creation all around us.

One of the most common arguments I encounter when discussing exercise with Christians is based on 1 Timothy 4:8 (KJV), which says, *"For bodily exercise profiteth little: but godliness is profitable unto all things, having promise of the life that now is, and of that which is to come."* This verse clearly stresses the priority godliness must have in our lives. While bodily exercise profits little compared with godliness, it is still of profit. Spiritual matters are of utmost importance, but I don't believe this verse condemns exercise. Our first priority must always be prayer and fellowship with the Lord, but I am convinced that our time with the Lord can be much more intimate when we are healthy in our bodies, souls and spirits. Your body is the temple of God, and when you exercise, you are caring for the temple and doing what you can to keep it healthy and strong for the service of the Lord. As I come into fellowship with the Lord each day, I am truly thankful to be living in the joy of His kingdom and for abundant health.

In order to fully understand 1Timothy 4:8, we must first consider the culture at the time it was written. During this time, lifestyles were very physical and active. Jesus and His disciples traveled primarily by foot through very rough and mountainous terrain. When they were in a hurry to get to their next destination before dark, I'm sure there were times when they even ran. Everyone in that day walked frequently and labored for even the bare necessities like water. Exercise for them wasn't something they had to make a concentrated effort to achieve.

In complete contrast, our modernized lifestyles don't require much physical activity at all. As a whole, we are a sedentary society, and we must make time to exercise our bodies because we were designed by God to move. Look at the shoulder and hip joints. They have an extremely wide range of motion because they were meant to be used.

All research agrees that exercise is imperative for a healthy body. So does it glorify God when we exercise? Certainly! It is our duty to take care of what has been entrusted to us. Without question, exercise will benefit us—body, soul and spirit.

Aerobic Exercise

Dr. Kenneth Cooper introduced the term *aerobics* more than thirty years ago to refer to movement that gets the heart and lungs working. He also discovered that there is a target heart rate to achieve optimal benefits from aerobic exercise. A person's target heart rate is determined by their maximum heart rate—how rapidly the heart is capable of beating per minute. It decreases with age and is approximately equal to 220 minus your age. A range of 60 to 80 percent of your maximum heart rate would be your target training heart rate. To reap the benefits of aerobic exercise, you must maintain your target heart rate for at least twenty minutes.

You can measure your own heart rate at the radial artery on your wrist or at the carotid artery on your neck. Take your index and middle fingers and gently press along the inside of your wrist a couple of inches below your thumb, or a few inches from the center of your neck—in the groove between your throat and the outer side. The easiest way to determine your heart rate is to count the number of beats in fifteen seconds, and then multiply that number by four. For example, if you count thirty beats in fifteen seconds, your heart rate would be one- hundred twenty beats per minutes (bpm). You can also tell if you are training at a good intensity if you can carry on a breathless conversation with someone. That means you are able to speak without having to stop for long pauses just to breathe.

We have found that our clients, who follow *The Trinity Diet* and lifestyle, have experienced significant health benefits from just thirty to forty-five minutes of even gentle to moderate walking each day. Because of the balance of macronutrients in their systems, they lose fat and often gain muscle by simply walking. When you exercise, your muscles use blood sugar for fuel. Additionally, exercise also helps to transport blood sugar into body cells keeping blood sugar and insulin in a healthy range. This type of physical activity helps a person to lose fat and gain muscle; it doesn't necessarily have to be strenuous. Of course, if you are already an athlete, you will need more than walking to maintain or grow your level of fitness. Regardless of where you are right now, make sure to vary the intensity of exercise according to your own fitness level.

For those of you just beginning, walking is a great functional exercise that everyone can do almost anywhere. Often, Amy and I go on a two-to-four-mile walk. It is at these times that we experience some of our most intimate fellowship with each other and the Lord. I remember one particular time when I was especially reluctant to go on a walk because I thought it would be boring. I am used to strenuous workouts, but to honor Amy, I agreed to go, and God really blessed our time together. We felt such a spirit of thankfulness for our lives and our many blessings that we just started thanking God for everything that came to our hearts: our health, our children, our home, our business, our family, friends, the beautiful trees, our neighbors and neighborhood, our church, and the list just kept going. I truly enjoyed it, much to my surprise. What a sweet time of fellowship with the Lord we had! We vowed to take walks as often as possible.

It is also important to do a variety of aerobic exercises to keep the heart and muscles challenged and to prevent boredom. Here is an assortment of possibilities:

- Walking
- Jogging
- Swimming
- Hiking
- Dancing
- Cardio kickboxing
- Circuit training
- Basketball
- Racquetball
- Tennis
- Bicycling, spinning or aerobic classes
- Working out on elliptical, stair or rowing machines

Another important benefit to keep in mind when considering fitness is that most diseases, including cancer, thrive in an anaerobic or no- oxygen environment. Studies have found that less than 17 percent of adults, who regularly exercise, get cancer. I believe this is due at least in part to the fact that the protein synthesis in a person who exercises, is improved through increased androgen hormones that allow for tissue building and repair.

The question about whether or not to exercise is truly a no-brainer.

Strength or Resistance Training

The word of God discusses how spiritual growth occurs when we go through the fire—this usually involves resistance. In our physical bodies, we grow in much the same way. With resistance, our muscles are built up. Metabolically active tissue grows and strengthens our bones. Just as exercise in general was a natural part of the culture and lifestyle of Jesus' day, so was strength training. Everyday tasks such as planting and harvesting crops, tending and feeding animals, washing clothes, and getting water from the river or a well, were only a few of the physically active, strengthening chores people performed as a part of daily life. A woman carrying a typical eight-gallon water jug on her head would be supporting at least eighty pounds of weight as she walked. Most ladies in today's world don't ever have to carry something that heavy. The women of biblical times however, did it every day.

When we increase our strength with resistance or weight training, we are increasing our skeletal muscle mass. This leads to a healthier countenance, increased energy and vitality, increased ability to perform everyday tasks that may have previously been difficult, and an increased BMR. When we don't use our muscles, they actually atrophy or waste away. This loss of lean body mass is referred to as sarcopenia, which literally means "loss of flesh."

As we age, we lose a certain amount of lean muscle mass and gain body fat. The average person loses about six and a half pounds of muscle per decade after the age twenty-five. By the age of sixty-five or seventy, the body may have doubled its fat mass and lost half its muscle mass. The speed at which this happens is strongly influenced by the consistency and intensity of strength training. Amy and I enjoy weight- resistance training four to six days per week, alternating body parts so that each muscle we work has one day to recover. Listen to your body, and if your are too sore from a previous workout, give the muscle an extra day before working it again. Based on this program, both of us have experienced an increase in muscle mass through the years.

As you can see, resistance or weight training is vital to sustaining muscle mass and it must be maintained to realize its full benefits. Strength exercises can be done at home or in a gym with free weights, your own body weight, or resistance machines. If you have never done resistance training, or if it has been a number of years since you did, we recommend that you work with a qualified personal trainer as you begin. This will ensure that you use proper form to avoid injury, and it will enable you to get the results you want.

Before working out with a trainer, please make sure that the person didn't just take a weekend course on the internet. Just as there is continual research in nutrition, there are also new studies on how to work out safely and wisely with weights. Therefore, it is important that you choose your trainer carefully. Women, you need to be cautious when training with a man, because you should not be working out like a man. For example, I saw a male trainer instructing a female client in her late forties, to perform dangerous power-lifting presses. There really is no reason a woman of that age should be doing that type of exercise. The possible minor benefits just don't outweigh the risks of injury.

Amy took a certification program to become a personal fitness instructor/trainer when she was in her mid-forties. I am so glad she did. She became acutely aware of how many people are injured while working out as a result from lack of instruction in proper form. Amy learned that correct form and posture are extremely important to prevent injury and gain desired results. Based on the knowledge she gained, we changed numerous things about our strength training workouts. When she trains ladies, especially those who are in their forties, fifties, and sixties, Amy always incorporates functional exercises that have movements we use in everyday life. Squats are very functional exercises because every day for the rest of your life, you will have to squat down on a toilet or chair. It's important to learn to do this properly in order to avoid back or knee injuries.

One of Amy's clients was a woman in her late fifties who had terrible knee pain. Every morning when she woke up, she dreaded the thought of sitting down on the toilet because it hurt her knees so much. She would back up to the toilet and just plop herself down. After Amy demonstrated the proper way to squat and had her perform it with a few sets of ten repetitions, her client was amazed that her knees no longer hurt when she sat down.

When we learn to strengthen our bodies with functional exercises, we will have the balance, agility, and coordination to keep us safe in all situations. If we find ourselves on a slick foor or icy sidewalk, our chances of righting ourselves when thrown off balance, and possibly preventing a serious injury, are much greater if we have exercised to strengthen ourselves. It is often common in youth not to think of these things, but as we age, we can experience a healthier life by keeping physically fit. It is one of the most important things we can do to ensure a longer, healthier life.

In addition to the benefits discussed so far, weight-resistance training is highly beneficial for bone health and heart strength. When you begin, I recommend hiring a personal trainer to learn safe techniques until you become comfortable with your knowledge. As a rule, you can gain better muscle tone and energy to last a lifetime with just twenty to thirty minutes of resistance training, three to four times a week. The father of fitness, Jack LaLanne, works out on weights for an hour every day and he's 95 years old. That's a pretty good living testimony. Amy lifts weights three or more times per week and is capable of squatting with a 135-pound barbell on her back. She is definitely one of the strongest women for her size and age. This should be the norm for society today, just as it was in biblical times.

No Excuses

Being physically active enables you to feel good and get more enjoyment out of life. It also prolongs life, improves mood, achieves metabolic balance, promotes fat loss, strengthens heart and blood vessels, increases bone density, decreases the incidences of illness and improves the immune system.

When we mention exercise to people, we often hear, "I'm too tired," or "I don't have enough time." Ironically, one of the reasons they are too tired is a lack of exercise! If we already know disease thrives in an anaerobic environment that lacks adequate oxygen, wisdom would say that we all need to exercise. In his book *The Miracle of Fasting,* Dr. Paul Bragg takes a strong stand for exercise saying, we earn our food with exercise [11] Paul says the same thing in scripture, *"If a man will not work, he shall not eat"* (2 Thess. 3:10). This makes sense on many levels. How many lions would catch a single gazelle after sitting on the couch for extended periods of time? Our bodies thrive on the same tension that exists in all creation—the same drama that has been playing out for centuries. Our bodies are made to be in motion. If God intended us to be stationary, He would not have made our bodies to move the way they do. Unfortunately, in our lives today, there is less and less need to move. We sit in cars, stand in elevators, and sit at computers all day. The less we move, the more immobile we become.

Flexibility

If you are having trouble reaching down to tie your shoes, or if it's getting harder for you to bend over to pick up something you have dropped, you probably need to improve your flexibility. Most of us lose flexibility as we age, but we can regain it. In this area, as in all areas of our lives, God is a God of restoration. Stretching on a daily basis will help to reduce muscle tension, prevent injuries, and increase your range of motion and coordination. Stretching also helps prepare our bodies for strenuous activity. When we exercise, the range of motion of our joints can decrease if we do not stretch, so it is always important to stretch before and after all aerobic and resistance exercise. However, be sure to warm up the muscles with a five-minute walk or bike ride before stretching. Cold muscles are hard to stretch, and this will warm them up and get blood flowing to the muscles. In addition to preventing injury, stretching elevates the supply of oxygen to your muscles and facilitates the removal of toxins.

As with all exercise, there is both a right and wrong way to stretch. Any time you stretch, you will want to follow these guidelines.

- Move slowly, and hold the stretch for at least twenty seconds.
- Hold stretches longer for larger muscles.
- Avoid bouncing, which increases the chance of injury.
- Breathe slowly and deeply from your diaphragm, making sure you don't hold your breath.
- Relax into the stretch, which over time will allow you to stretch farther.

- Listen to your body. Stretching should not be painful, and overstretching can cause injury.
- Do not overstretch if you are pregnant.
- Stretch all muscle groups regularly.

Maintenance

Today at age fifty-four, I continue to set goals to help me maintain the strength of my youth. I believe we should always have a goal before us whether it concerns our walk with the Lord, exercise, menu planning, marriage, relationships, or business. Goals are important in all areas of our lives! We know our bodies will die, but a healthy and fit body while still alive, will yield the greatest return, helping us to fulfill God's callings throughout a lifetime.

As you develop and maintain healthy fitness habits, may these Bible verses encourage you to keep reaching toward God's best for you.

"Now may the God of peace Himself sanctify you completely; and may your whole spirit, soul, and body be preserved blameless at the coming of our Lord Jesus Christ." (I Thess. 5:23 NKJV)

"We pray this in order that you may live a life worthy of the Lord and may please him in every way: bearing fruit in every good work, growing in the knowledge of God, being strengthened with all power according to his glorious might so that you may have great endurance and patience, and joyfully giving thanks to the Father, who has qualified you to share in the inheritance of the saints in the Kingdom of light. For he has rescued us from the dominion of darkness and brought us into the kingdom of the Son he loves." (Col. 1:10-13)

"I can do all things through Christ who strengthens me." (Phil. 4:13 NKJV)

"But those who wait on the LORD Shall renew [their] strength; They shall mount up with wings like eagles, They shall run and not be weary, They shall walk and not faint." (Is. 40:31 NKJV)

CHAPTER 10

MAKING IT WORK
FOR YOU

"Or don't you know that your body is the temple of the Holy Spirit, who lives in you and was given to you by God? You do not belong to yourself, for God bought you with a high price. So you must honor God with your body."
I CORINTHIANS 6:19-20 (NLT)

MAKING A lifestyle change is difficult, even for those of us who are motivated to do so. When people cannot immediately see the benefits of action, they frequently resist it. You may experience this resistance from your spouse, your children, your extended family, and even your friends. Remember, Rome was not built in a day! You may have to take time to educate and remind your family and others about what you're doing and why. It takes time to build something great that will be remembered and is worthwhile.

Parents keep in mind, it is our responsibility to train up our children in the way they should go both spiritually and physically. They are watching us, so be good examples for them by feeding your temples correctly. This is pleasing to the Lord—an act of worship unto Him.

Our children learned how to take care of their bodies in our home when they were young. Today as adults, they incorporate these same principles into their own lives and homes. The truths that we taught them then, will further effect another generation. Their children, spouses and friends will all be positively impacted.

One of the most important things you can do as you get started with your *Trinity Diet*, is to sit down with your family and explain the reasons for the changes you are implementing. Explain that you want to obey God and walk closer to Him so that there will be less sickness and fewer trips to the doctor. Tell them it may be difficult, and then encourage them that they can do all things through Christ who strengthens all of us.

Ten Steps for Making the Transition

Here are ten steps to help you and your family transition to healthier eating habits and a healthier lifestyle.

1. Stop or slow down the purchase of junk food. When it is not readily available, it will be easier to eat less junk and try alternatives.
2. Make sure each meal has a balance of *The Trinity Diet* macronutrients: protein (the Father), carbohydrates (the Son) and fats (the Holy Spirit).
3. Pray before your meal that the Lord would strengthen your body for the works of service to which He has called you.
4. Use missed opportunities for good choices as teachable moments. Children and others learn from example. When they make bad choices, teach them how they could have made a different choice to produce a better result.
5. Take responsibility for the way you and your family eat. Plan ahead so you aren't tempted to excuse bad choices because it was the only food available. (When we go to dinner or church meetings where food is being served, we often bring a medical food shake just in case there are not enough nutrients available.)
6. Make meals a positive family time, remembering that Jesus is always present at the table.
7. Do not allow the dinner table to become a battlefield. Dismiss children to another room if they do not behave.
8. Only buy foods you want your family to eat.
9. Do not let your children decide what foods to buy at the grocery store unless they are choosing healthy foods. Make a list before you go, and stick to it as close as possible.
10. Do not feel deprived. There are healthy alternatives to all junk foods. Educate yourself and your family as to why one is better than the other. Be sure to go to health food stores and try new things for variety.

Other Suggestions

Here are a few other suggestions that will help you as you embrace the *Trinity Diet* lifestyle:

1. Avoid sugar or simple carbohydrates (white bread, pasta, and cereals). These are also known as refined carbohydrates.
2. Avoid dairy products (see www.not.milk.com for overwhelming reasons to avoid dairy).
3. Avoid soft drinks. Drink only water or herbal teas.
4. Incorporate good fats into your diet. Eliminate animal and processed fats, such as lard, margarine, and fatty meats, and avoid hydrogenated oils in packaged products.
5. Eat organically grown food whenever possible.
6. Avoid caffeine. It is an alkaloid chemical that is toxic to our bodies in excess and depletes our energy reserves.
7. Never skip meals unless God has called you to a fast. Eat every three to four hours to maintain optimal energy and keep stable blood sugar levels.
8. Avoid packaged and processed foods whenever possible.
9. Read nutrition labels carefully to avoid sugar, corn syrup, hydrogenated fats, and long, hard to pronounce ingredients that are usually chemicals. Products with fewer ingredients are usually purer, more natural foods.

Trinity Cycles of the Body

In a twenty-four-hour period, the body goes through three different cycles, each with a specific function. Detoxification begins in the morning to assist the removal of toxic exposure each day. The assimilation cycle takes over next for the intake of nutrients. This is when digestion breaks down your food into molecules, such as amino acids from protein and fatty acids from fats, creating usable components to facilitate bodily functions. During the evening and night hours, the restorative cycle starts to rebuild tissues.

The following is a typical day broken down into the trinity of cycles:

1. Detoxification cycle –

Each morning, be sure to allow adequate time to break from overnight fasting before you begin your activities for the day. This is where the word 'breakfast' gets its meaning. I take this time to read the word, pray, worship God, and nourish my body to cleanse.

The most active period for the body to cleanse is between 4 a.m. and 12 p.m. These hours between rising and eating lunch, provide a good time to consume foods such as fruits, melons, water, green drinks, juices, and smoothies which support cleansing. As you do this, you may have several bowel movements allowing the body to remove the waste material accumulated from the previous day.

I consume a variety of herbs and almost two quarts of water in the first four to four and a half hours after waking up in order to facilitate the detoxification cycle and hydrate the body. During this time, I usually have three or more bowel movements. Between waking and eating lunch, I will consume two separate medical food shakes with fruit and oils that support the detoxification cycle as well. I also utilize some of the herbal nutrition outlined in *Chapter Seven* to support the detoxification cycle.

2. Assimilation cycle –

After the early morning hours give way to lunchtime, the assimilation cycle begins. This time between 11 a.m. and 6 p.m. is the best time for the body to take in the largest amounts of food and nutrients. You may find that consuming a large meal at lunch will prevent the fatigue that tends to come when you wait too long to eat. I usually eat a meat, legumes, avocado salad with olive oil, and rarely, a rice or sweet potato around 12:30 pm.

About three hours after you eat lunch is a good time to take another medical food shake or other snack with adequate nutrients. Then try to eat dinner between 6 p.m. and 7 p.m.

My dinner usually consists of salad, protein, legumes, and a vegetable. In addition to your morning meal and shake, this completes five meals consumed between 6 a.m. and 7 p.m.

3. Restoration cycle –

It is best not to eat after 7 p.m. or 8 p.m. when the body is ready to utilize the nutrients to restore, rebuild, and repair cellular tissue damage that has occurred during the day.

During deep REM sleep, the body secretes growth hormone to allow for complete restoration, and eating too late can disturb the delicate sleep cycle. When we consume excess calories late in the day, the body lacks the energy to digest food into smaller, usable molecules which are so necessary for it. The undigested components of food then continue into the digestive tract causing irritation to the intestinal lining and confusing the immune system into attacking these undigested molecules. This phenomenon is known as auto-immune reaction. Upon waking the next day, you may notice you feel stiff, fatigued, or achy, and you may even suffer from sinus irritation, headaches, and drainage.

Pay careful attention to how late you eat, and you will feel more refreshed in the morning. Before bed, you can take additional calcium, magnesium, potassium, and trace minerals to help alkalize the body and relax your muscles for the purpose of gaining better sleep.

Chapter Eight has additional information on herbal supports that may be specifically helpful to you before bed. We take minerals to help with sleep and herbs in small quantities to support immune strength, aid in adrenal and intestinal detoxification, and to assist with hormone balance for restful sleep.

Store Up Treasure

Like King Solomon, we should desire knowledge and understanding more than silver or gold. In Hosea 4:6, the Lord stresses through his prophet, *"My people are destroyed from lack of knowledge."* When we study to show ourselves approved to God, we will not be ashamed. Educating yourself in health will encourage you to forgo your former lifestyle, just as the people of Israel learned more about God and forsook the former ways they'd learned in Egypt. If we return to eating processed foods, fried foods, hydrogenated oils, soft drinks, acidic coffee and medications, then the pain and suffering from the past will soon return.

As a family, a large amount of our "treasure" is spent on health. This is so because we believe our bodies to be the temples of the Living God which should be built up. We purchase high-quality supplements and herbs, organic foods whenever possible, and natural meats without hormones and chemicals. As we seek to put only the best choices into our bodies—as is only fitting for God's temple, we trust Him to supply our every need, the same way He did for the building of the Temple in Jerusalem. Jesus said, *"For where your treasure is, there your heart will be also"* (Matt. 6:21). When we spend our treasure to support our bodies, we are in fact building "living temples" of God under the new covenant and can be assured that God will always provide for His temple. When Solomon built the Temple in his day, the Lord blessed him in many ways because of his desire to please God and to help people. God will do the same for us.

When Amy was pregnant with our youngest daughter Mikala, we decided she would stay home and school our children in a God-fearing atmosphere. I remember crying out in prayer with Amy that the Lord would help us financially, and that our body and health convictions would not be compromised. We felt that our health was a reflection of God's mighty hand of healing and prosperity, and knew He would hear and answer our request. God provided in every way! The Lord was faithful, blessing us and our children with good health. For a number of years, we only bought things for our home and family at garage sales. We found great joy when we were able to hand down our garage sale clothes to friends, for their children. What a blessing the act of giving brings! On two separate occasions, different women approached Amy and told her that the Lord had spoken to them to give her clothing including shoes, shirts, jewelry, pants, and even dresses. The Lord provided above and beyond our needs at exactly the time we needed it. It was in this season that we began receiving invitations to speak on health at churches and to groups, the Lord was so good, even providing Amy with nice clothing to stand before God's people.

We must act according to God's promises. He is watching to see His word fulfilled (Jer. 1:12) because He delights in the power of His word. If you want that power in your life, you must heed the word of God. I Samuel 15:22 says, *"To obey is better than sacrifice."*

Temporary Afflictions

Whenever we make the choice to line our lives up in obedience to the word of God, we can expect temporary Afflictions. As the Israelites began their journey of freedom from Egypt to the Promised Land, they quickly ran into problems. Food and water became scarce, and the people doubted Moses' decisions and his authority to lead them. Psalm 106:13-15 tells us, *"But they soon forgot what he had done and did not wait for his counsel.*

In the desert they gave in to their craving; in the wasteland they put God to the test. So he gave them what they asked for, but sent a wasting disease upon them."

People, who begin to make changes in their health patterns, will often experience difficulties as the Israelites did after their departure from Egypt. As our bodies begin flushing out toxins, multiple symptoms may occur—pain, fever, fatigue, and mental confusion. This might tempt us to return to old habits. When you struggle with these symptoms, wait on God and trust Him for the healing to come. If you are able to persevere through these temporary struggles, you will be less likely to run back to your old lifestyle. Unfortunately, those unwilling to change will probably suffer with disease one day.

My Mother's Transformation

My own mother Dorothy, has an amazing testimony of how God blessed her willingness to embrace and stick to a *Trinity Diet* lifestyle. Her favorite pass-time is enjoying the beauty of God's creation on the golf course. She has always been a champion golfer and has won women's club championships many times through the years. In recent years, she started having back pain and fatigue that would not allow her to enjoy golf without discomfort and pain. For many years, she continued to gain weight and diminish in health, but when she made a few simple lifestyle changes, she was able to have a healthier body. As my mom learned to balance her food intake, she applied *The Trinity Diet* principles and found renewed vitality. She shares:

> I am 72 years old, and the mother of the nutritionist who wrote *The Trinity Diet*. In January of 2008, I few to Houston to visit Steve at his health clinic. They proceeded to perform testing to evaluate the health of my body. From the testing and consultation time, he developed a balanced food and nutritional supplement program for me. After six months, I lost thirty-six pounds and felt so much better. My energy level increased, and I felt like a new person. I have received many compliments on my appearance. I couldn't have done it without his help and support. Many thanks to him; He changed my life.

Now, mother and dad have to find younger friends who can keep up with their active lifestyle. She is proof of Haggai 2:9, which says:

> *"The future glory of this Temple will be greater than the past glory, says the LORD Almighty; And in this place I will bring peace."* Jesus said in John 16:33, *"These things I have spoken to you, so that in me you may have peace. In the world you have tribulation, but take courage; I have overcome the world."*

As we have established, the bodies in which we live are the temples of God. God promises that the power that lives in you is able to overcome the destruction and dangers in this world. In addition, the glory of the temple—your body, can be greater in the latter days.

You get to choose! You can choose to be an over-comer by following the Lord's pattern for healthy living. Allow His wisdom to transform what you believe and walk by faith in the newness of life that He provides. We have done our best to make the steps in this book simple. The following "Checklist of a Healthy Human" should motivate you to run the race of health leading to a strong and disease- free lifestyle. We really do know from experience that implementing the simple truths of *The Trinity Diet* will allow you to live the abundant life Jesus promised.

Years from now, you too will look back and see how the hand of God has delivered you and your family from disease just as He has proclaimed, *"I will put none of the diseases upon you"* (Ex. 15:26 NKJV). As you are obedient to care for the temple and live *The Trinity Diet*, He will reward you as He has us.

Checklist of a Healthy Human

Check each item below that applies to you to determine your current level of health. Total the number of checks at the bottom to find out where you stand as a healthy human.

1. _____ Ideal body weight for height

2. _____ Solid, lean muscle with optimal fat ratio

3. _____ No weakness or fatigue

4. _____ Bright eyes; whites not blood shot

5. _____ Absence of disease or illness

6. _____ Quick-healing injuries and sickness Clear, soft, and smooth skin

7. _____ Absence of body odor

8. _____ Cravings only for nature's food

9. _____ Lack of desire for toxic foods and substances

10. _____ Cleansing reactions such as vomiting, diarrhea and fever, etc. when toxic foods are consumed

11. _____ Regular bowel movements daily (three or more per day)

12. _____ Fruity or no stool odor

13. _____ Stool floats and is soft and easy to eliminate

14. _____ Urine not too strong in odor with a golden sunshine yellow color

15. _____ Saliva pH of 7.0 or higher

16. _____ No fatigue, only drowsiness at bedtime

17. _____ Rest and sleep peacefully

18. _____ Awaken with energy, feeling refreshed

19. _____ Enthusiastic about life

20. _____ Able to handle stress in proper perspective without losing your cool

21. _____ A sense of fulfillment and accomplishment at the end of each day

22. _____ Love, forgiveness, and acceptance of self and others

23. _____ Living in righteousness, peace, and joy each day

24. _____ Exercise four times per week for forty minutes without feeling of fatigued

_____ Total numbers checked

Find your score below to see how you rate.

5 or less	You need to consider serious lifestyle changes.
5 to 10	You are trying to stay out of trouble most of the time.
10 to 15	You are on your way to living the dream.
15 to 20	Your are a seriously committed health advocate.
20 to 25	You are living an abundant healthy life for God.

THE TRINITY
DIET KITCHEN

"Let me prepare some food to refresh you. Please stay awhile before continuing on your journey."
GENESIS 18:5 (NLT)

P ART OF making the *Trinity Diet* work for you, is to stock up your pantry and refrigerator with the right staples and ingredients. You also need to have the right tools to simplify food preparation and cooking. Now add to that some really great recipes, and I believe you will quickly find yourself ready and able to sustain your new *Trinity Diet* lifestyle.

Getting Equipped in the Kitchen

We're about to take the old adage, "The tools make the man," to a whole new level. Having the right tools in the kitchen is just as important as having the right tools in the garage. As you read through this chapter, keep in mind that you can build your kitchen over time. It does not have to be done overnight. Avoid feeling pressured to run out and buy all sorts of gadgets, when you can start small, and add as you go. As you begin to outfit your kitchen, pace yourself, and be sure to research different brands. Try new recipes, and see what becomes important to you. When purchasing counter appliances, consider:

- your counter space
- storage space
- the quality and durability of the appliance

Prices will vary greatly, and sometimes saving up for the right appliance is better than getting average use from an average appliance.

Tools of the Trade

Here are some of the items we have found to be most useful in our kitchen. This is a great place to start as you equip your kitchen.

1. Blender for preparing smoothies, dressings, nut milks, and fruit beverages
2. Juicer for making your own fresh fruit and vegetable juices
3. Garlic press
4. Toaster
5. Water purification system
6. Mini or hand chopper
7. Salad spinner
8. Stainless steel cookware
9. At least one really good knife

Seasonings and Condiments

We regularly use the following staples and seasonings in our cooking. These items will help you create delicious, healthy meals:

Organic apple cider vinegar
Bragg's Liquid Aminos
Cinnamon
Fresh and dried ginger
Organic ketchup
Red miso
Sea or Celtic sea salt
Various herbs, fresh or dried

Balsamic vinegar
Cayenne
Fresh garlic
Fresh lemon
Organic mustard
Safflower mayonnaise
Tahini (ground sesame)

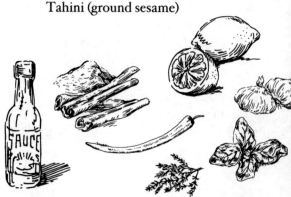

Sweeteners

Choosing healthy, natural sweeteners is of utmost importance. Be sure to try several to find the one that best satisfies your palette.

Cane sugar
Maple syrup
Molasses
Date sugar
Stevia (powder and liquid)

Honey
Sucanat
Rice syrup
Agave nectar

Oils

Extra virgin olive oil
Flax oil
High oleic safflower oil

RECIPES
SALADS

Lentil Salad (4-6 servings)

2 cups lentils, rinsed
3½ cups water
2-3 tablespoons balsamic vinegar
1/3 cup olive oil
2 garlic cloves, minced
2 teaspoons dried basil
1 small red onion, finely chopped

½ cup black olives, chopped
½ cup carrots, shredded
2 medium tomatoes, chopped
1 medium bell pepper, chopped
1 cup fresh parsley, chopped
¼ teaspoon ground black pepper
1 teaspoon fine sea salt

Simmer lentils, covered in water, about 30 to 45 minutes, until tender. Drain and cool. Combine vinegar, olive oil, garlic, basil, salt, and pepper in a jar, and mix well. Combine remaining ingredients with lentils, and toss with dressing. Refrigerate for one hour and serve.

Tuna Salad with Tomato, Avocado and Olives (2-4 servings)

2 (6-ounce) cans white albacore tuna fish in water
2 tablespoons Dijon mustard
¼ cup scallions, chopped
½ avocado, chopped
1 cup lettuce, chopped
½ cup kalamata olives, pitted and chopped

¼ cup mayonnaise
¼ cup celery, chopped
5 cherry tomatoes, halved
¼ cup veggie cheese

Drain tuna, and mix first four ingredients together. Season with salt and pepper. Arrange lettuce on plate, and top with tuna, tomatoes, olives, avocado, and cheese.

Quinoa Salad (12 servings)

1½ cups quinoa, rinsed well
3 cups vegetable broth or water
1 red bell pepper, diced
¼ cup parsley, chopped
½ cup Basic Salad Dressing (see recipe in Dressing section)

¼ cup red onion, diced
3 scallions, thinly sliced
¼ cup fresh dill, chopped
1 cup frozen baby peas, thawed

Add quinoa to broth or water in medium saucepan. Stir, and bring to a boil. Reduce to simmer, and then cover and cook 15 minutes without stirring or until liquid is absorbed. Remove ingredients from saucepan, and place in bowl. Cool slightly, and toss with salad dressing and remaining ingredients. Add more dressing if desired, and adjust seasoning to taste. Any leftover veggie can be added for variety.

Red Pepper and Zucchini Salad (4-6 servings)

2 sweet red peppers
2 zucchini
1 tablespoon olive oil
1 clove garlic, crushed

2 tablespoons wine vinegar
1-2 teaspoons Bragg's Liquid Aminos
¼ cup sesame seeds
Salt and pepper to taste

Wash peppers and zucchini. Slice peppers into 1-inch strips. Cut ends off zucchini, quarter lengthwise, and chop into 1-inch pieces. Sauté zucchini in 1 tablespoon olive oil for 4 to 5 minutes, until lightly browned and just soft. Add garlic, and stir for 30 seconds, then stir in peppers. Stir fry for 3 to 5 more minutes. Toss the sauté with vinegar and soy sauce. Marinate 6 hours or overnight. Season with salt and pepper to taste, and toss with sesame seeds before serving.

Red Potato and Green Bean Salad (4- 6 servings)

4 medium red potatoes, cooked
2 teaspoons balsamic vinegar
2 garlic cloves, slivered
1 tablespoon fresh oregano, chopped
1 tablespoon fresh basil, chopped
Salt and pepper to taste

2-4 tablespoons olive or flaxseed oil
¼-½ cup red onion, thinly sliced
1 pound fresh green beans, steamed

Combine beans with olive or flaxseed oil, vinegar, onion, garlic, basil, and oregano. Add salt and pepper to taste. Mix all ingredients together (except for potatoes), and chill. Just before serving, add warm potatoes to cold salad.

Carrot Salad (4 servings)

2 cups carrots, shredded
¼ cup sunflower seeds
2 tablespoons pineapple juice

½ cup celery, diced
3-4 tablespoons coconut milk

Mix together, and chill for 2 to 3 hours before serving.

Red Cabbage Salad (4 servings)

1 medium head red cabbage, coarsely chopped
10 radishes, sliced
3 tart apples, diced
1 stalk celery, chopped
Dash garlic powder
1 tablespoon balsamic vinegar

2 green onions, chopped
¼ cup walnuts, chopped
1-2 tablespoons lemon juice to taste
2 tablespoons olive oil

Mix everything in bowl, and let sit for 1 hour, stirring once or twice.

Tropical Salad (4-6 servings)

1 avocado, cubed
8 pineapple slices, cubed
1 papaya or mango, cubed

½ cup celery, diced
½ cup mango or pineapple juice

Combine all ingredients, and garnish with fresh mint leaves.

Chicken Salad Oriental (4 servings)

¼ cup olive oil
2 tablespoons seasoned rice vinegar
1 tablespoon Bragg's Liquid Aminos
¼ pound Chinese pea pods, cut in half
3 cups coleslaw mix
1 cup chicken, cooked and diced
½ cup almonds, sliced

Mix oil, vinegar, and Bragg's in large bowl. Add remaining ingredients, and toss to coat. Serve immediately.

Black Bean Salad (6-8 servings)

2 cans organic black beans, drained   1 cup cherry tomatoes
¼ cup red onion, chopped   ½ cup bell pepper, chopped
1 tablespoon olive oil   1-2 teaspoons cumin
1 teaspoon lemon juice or balsamic vinegar

Mix ingredients together in a bowl, and chill for several hours.

Guacamole Salad (4 servings)

2-3 ripe avocadoes   Juice of one lemon
½ cup picante sauce
2 tablespoons Amy's Sensational Sauce (see recipe under Miscellaneous)

Blend avocadoes in mini-chopper, blender, or food processor. Spoon remaining ingredients, and stir well.

Curried Chicken Salad (4 servings)

2½ pounds boneless, skinless white meat chicken, cooked and diced
½ cup mango or papaya juice   1 cup red and green apple, diced
¼ teaspoon turmeric   1 tablespoon olive oil
2 stalks celery, diced   ½ small jicama, peeled and diced
1 teaspoon curry powder   Salt and pepper to taste

Bake chicken at 350°F for 20 minutes, then dice. Place cooked, diced chicken in large salad bowl and cool. Combine with remaining ingredients. Adjust seasoning to taste, and refrigerate for an hour before serving.

DRESSINGS

Amy's Super Salad Dressing (6-8 servings)

1/3 cup safflower mayonnaise
2 tablespoons organic ketchup
¼ cup organic apple cider vinegar
¼ cup olive oil
4-5 cloves garlic, pressed or minced
2-3 tablespoons Bragg's Liquid Aminos

3-4 tablespoons tahini (ground sesame)
2 tablespoons organic mustard
¼ cup balsamic vinegar
¼ cup fax oil
½ cup water

Put as many ingredients as you have on hand directly into blender. (You don't have to have all of the above ingredients. You can actually use about half of them and still have a great salad dressing.) Blend until thoroughly mixed. Increase or decrease ingredients to your personal taste. Serve on salad, potatoes, rice, or pasta.

Balsamic/Mustard Vinaigrette (4 servings)

¼ cup each fax oil and olive oil
3 tablespoons balsamic vinegar
1 teaspoon Dijon mustard

1-3 cloves fresh garlic, chopped
2-3 tablespoons water
Salt and pepper to taste Oregano,

basil, parsley, tarragon, or any herbs of your liking, fresh or dried (oregano and basil are typical of Italian dressings)

In a jar with a secure lid, add vinegar, water, and mustard. Shake well to thoroughly dissolve mustard. Add oil and remaining ingredients, and shake well. Amounts can be adjusted to taste. Store in refrigerator. Take out 5 to 10 minutes before using so dressing can re-liquefy (it will harden when refrigerated). Shake well before using.

Tofu Mayonnaise (4-6 servings)

½ pound tofu
¼ cup lemon juice
½ cup safflower oil

½ teaspoon sea salt
1 teaspoon dry mustard

Blend all ingredients in blender until thick. Store in refrigerator, or it can be frozen and defrosted for use at a later time.

Tahini Dressing (6 servings)

6 tablespoons sesame tahini   Lemon juice to taste

Mix tahini with lemon juice, and add water until desired consistency for salad dressing.

Ranch-Type Dressing (4-6 servings)

¾ cup low-fat plain yogurt   ¼ cup buttermilk
1 tablespoon grated onion   1 tablespoon lemon juice
Pinches of oregano and cayenne pepper
1 teaspoon vegetable seasoning mix (Spike has a good one)

Combine all ingredients in bowl, and stir with fork (this dressing will get too thin if mixed in blender or food processor). Store in refrigerator.

Russian Dressing (2-4 servings)

1-2 tablespoons Ranch-Type Dressing   1-2 tablespoons salsa

Stir ingredients together, and serve.

Flax Oil Dressing (4-6 servings)

¼ cup fax oil   1-3 cloves fresh garlic
¼ cup olive oil   3 tablespoons balsamic vinegar
2-3 tablespoons water   1 teaspoon Dijon mustard Oregano,
basil, parsley, tarragon, or any herbs, fresh or dried
Salt and pepper to taste

In a jar with a secure lid, add vinegar, water, and mustard. Shake well to thoroughly dissolve mustard. Add oil and remaining ingredients, and shake well. Amounts can be adjusted to taste. Store in refrigerator. Take out 5 to 10 minutes before using so dressing can re-liquefy (it will harden when refrigerated). Shake well before using.

Creamy Vinaigrette Dressing (4-6 servings)

Mix equal amounts of Flax Oil Dressing and Ranch-Type Dressing, and serve.

SOUPS & STEWS

Lentil-Barley Stew (8 servings)

2 tablespoons olive oil
4 medium carrots, diced
2 medium leeks, diced
7 cups chicken or vegetable broth
2 celery stalks, diced
2 medium zucchini, diced
1 large onion, diced
Salt and pepper to taste

1 teaspoon dried thyme
1 cup dried lentils, rinsed
½ cup barley
2 cups tomatoes, diced
1 cup fresh basil leaves, chopped
½ cup parsley, chopped
1 garlic clove, minced

Heat olive oil in large, heavy pot, and add carrots, leeks, celery, zucchini, onion, and garlic. Cook over low heat, stirring occasionally for about 10 minutes until vegetables have softened. Add lentils, barley, thyme, and 6 cups of broth. Bring to a boil, and reduce heat to a simmer. Cook uncovered about 30 minutes, stirring often. Add remaining cup of broth as needed if dry. Add tomatoes, basil, and salt and pepper to taste. Continue cooking 10 more minutes. Stir in parsley and serve.

Amy's Lentil Soup (6-8 servings)

8 cups cold water
4 tablespoons Bragg's Liquid Aminos
3-4 cloves of garlic
½ teaspoon cayenne
2½ cup rinsed lentils (red and/or green)
1 (16-ounce) can tomatoes or tomato sauce
3 cups red or green cabbage, chopped

1-2 stalks celery
½ teaspoon oregano
1 teaspoon sea salt
2 cups carrots, grated

Combine all ingredients in soup pot. Bring to a boil, reduce heat, and simmer 1½ hours. Add water if it is too thick. Add more Bragg's to taste.

Quinoa Vegetable Soup (4-6 servings)

¼ cup quinoa (well rinsed) 2 teaspoons olive oil
½ cup carrots, diced 4 cups water
¼ cup celery, diced ½ cup tomato, chopped
2 tablespoons onion, chopped ½ cup cabbage, chopped
¼ cup green pepper, diced ¼ cup fresh parsley, chopped
2 cloves garlic, chopped Salt and pepper to taste

Sauté quinoa, carrots, celery, onion, green bell pepper, and garlic in oil until softened. Add water, tomato, and cabbage. Bring to a boil. Simmer 20 to 30 minutes or until tender. Season to taste, and garnish with parsley. For variations, add other vegetables, chopped and sautéed.

Autumn Bean Soup (6 servings)

2 cups white kidney beans, cooked   2 onions, chopped
1 cup red beans, cooked   2 cloves garlic, minced
1 cup chickpeas, cooked   1 teaspoon dried basil
2-3 cups fresh spinach, chopped   1 tablespoon dried parsley
4 cups chicken broth   Pepper to taste
Parmesan cheese (optional)   1 teaspoon dried oregano

Combine all ingredients, and simmer until onions are soft, about 45 minutes. Garnish with parmesan cheese (optional).

Lentil Soup (4 servings)

2 garlic cloves, minced   2 quarts water or broth
1 medium onion, chopped   Salt to taste
2 celery stalks, chopped   Pinch thyme or preferred seasoning
2 large carrots, sliced   ½ cup red and/or green lentils

Combine first five ingredients, and bring to a boil. Add seasonings and lentils. Reduce heat to medium-low, and simmer (covered) for 45 minutes to 1 hour (until lentils are soft). Puree half in the blender for a creamy soup.

133

Barley Minestrone Soup (8 servings)

1 tablespoon olive oil
1 medium onion, chopped
2 stalks celery, diced
3 carrots, sliced or diced
2 cloves garlic, minced
1 pound fresh green beans cut into one-inch pieces

1 (28-ounce) can tomatoes with juice
1/3 cup whole barley
1 bay leaf
1 (16-ounce) can kidney beans, drained
6 cups chicken stock

In heavy 6-quart pot, sauté onion, celery, carrot, and garlic in oil until just softened. Add stock, tomatoes, barley, and bay leaf. Bring to a boil and cover, reducing heat to a simmer for 50 minutes, stirring occasionally. Stir in kidney beans and green beans, and simmer for 5 to 10 minutes more until all vegetables are tender. Remove bay leaf and serve.

Split Pea Soup (10 servings)

3 cups split peas, rinsed
1 bay leaf
8 cups chicken broth or water
1 teaspoon mustard powder
Salt and pepper to taste

3 stalks celery, chopped
3 medium carrots, dices
2 cloves garlic, minced
1 large onion, chopped

In a 6-quart pot, combine peas, desired liquid, and bay leaf. Bring to a boil, lower heat, and simmer for 20 minutes, stirring occasionally. Add remaining ingredients, and continue to simmer for 40 additional minutes, stirring occasionally. Add salt and pepper to taste.

Creamy Cold Tomato Soup (5 servings)

1 cucumber, chopped
1 scallion, chopped
1 clove garlic
1 cup plain yogurt
Sliced mushrooms or tomatoes for garnish

1 green pepper, chopped
½ teaspoon dill weed
4 cups tomato juice

Combine all ingredients (except yogurt) in small amounts in blender, and blend until smooth. Use salt sparingly, if needed, and pepper. Whisk in yogurt. Chill several hours before serving, and garnish as desired with mushrooms or tomatoes.

MAIN DISHES

Fish Creole (4 servings)

1 tablespoon olive oil
1 onion, chopped
½ cup celery, thinly sliced
¼ cup green pepper, chopped
1 garlic clove, minced
2 tablespoons fresh parsley

1 bay leaf
¼ teaspoon rosemary, chopped
1 (28-ounce) can tomatoes with liquid
1 pound fish filets
2 cups brown rice, cooked

Heat oil in large saucepan, and lightly sauté onion, celery, pepper, and garlic until soft. Add parsley, bay leaf, rosemary, and tomatoes. Simmer, uncovered, about 20 minutes. Add fish fillets in small pieces, and simmer until cooked through, about 5 to 10 minutes. Remove bay leaf. Serve over brown rice.

Poached Salmon with Dill (4 servings)

2 cups chicken broth
½ cucumber, peeled and sliced
1 cup wild rice, cooked
2 tablespoons dill, chopped
¾ pound salmon fillet, skinned and cut into 4 pieces

½ cup dry white wine
1 teaspoon grated lemon zest
½ medium avocado, diced
¼ teaspoon freshly ground pepper

In large skillet, bring broth and wine to a boil. Add cucumber and lemon zest, then reduce heat, and simmer until cucumber is tender, about 2 minutes. Stir in rice, avocado, dill, and pepper, and then add salmon. Poach, covered, until fish is opaque in the center (4 to 6 minutes).

Walnut Chicken Breast Stir Fry (4 servings)

5 tablespoons olive oil	6 teaspoons Bragg's Liquid Aminos
½ teaspoon ground ginger	1 red bell pepper
½ cup walnuts, chopped	½ teaspoon garlic, minced
1 medium onion, chopped	½ cup chicken broth
1 cup broccoli flowerets	1 green bell pepper
4 cups assorted greens	
4 chicken breasts, boneless and skinless	

In large bowl, combine 2 tablespoons olive oil and 3 teaspoons Bragg's. Set aside. Cut peppers and onion into 1-inch pieces. Cut chicken breasts into 1-inch pieces. Add chicken to large bowl, and stir to coat. Cover and place in refrigerator for 30 minutes. While waiting, combine ginger, chicken broth, and remaining Bragg's. In large skillet or wok, heat remaining olive oil over medium heat (but not smoking). Add chicken (discard extra marinade), and cook until no longer pink. Remove chicken, and stir-fry onion and peppers until onion is tender. Add broccoli, and cook until tender. Add chicken and broth mixture, stirring constantly until evenly heated. Turn off heat, add walnuts, and stir. On four serving plates, divide mixed greens evenly, and then pour walnut chicken mixture onto center of greens.

Tuna-Almond Casserole (2-4 servings)

½ cup onion, chopped	¼ cup cold-pressed olive oil
½ green pepper, chopped	½ cup almonds, slivered
1 (8-ounce) can water-packed tuna, drained	

In skillet, lightly sauté onion, bell pepper, and ¼ cup almonds in olive oil. Combine with tuna. Put in casserole dish, and cover with remaining almonds. Bake 15 min at 4250F.

Crustless Vegetable Quiche (6 servings)

5 eggs	10 ounces frozen chopped broccoli
½ cup rice milk	10 ounces frozen chopped spinach
¾ cup cottage cheese	1 tablespoon olive oil
½ cup grated vegetable cheese	Salt and pepper to taste

Beat eggs in medium-sized bowl. Add milk, and beat some more. Add remaining ingredients, and stir vigorously to blend. Pour into deep, lightly oiled casserole dish. Place casserole dish in 9x13-inch pan partially filled with hot water. Bake at 375°F for about 35 to 45 minutes or until a knife inserted into quiche comes out clean.

Roasted Red Snapper with Salsa (8 servings)

4 red snapper fillets, 8 ounces each
1 tablespoon fresh lime juice
Salt and pepper to taste Salsa (recipe below)
4 teaspoons olive oil
1 tablespoon fresh cilantro, chopped

Preheat oven to 400°F. Brush 1 teaspoon olive oil on baking sheet. Place fish on baking sheet, skin side down. Combine remaining olive oil, lime juice, and cilantro, and brush on each fillet. Sprinkle with salt and pepper to taste. Allow to sit for 15 minutes. Bake for 20 minutes or until just cooked. Serve immediately.

Salsa (2-4 servings)

2 large tomatoes, diced
1 tablespoon chopped cilantro
1 tablespoon olive oil
2 scallions, chopped
1 clove garlic, crushed
2 teaspoons fresh lime juice

Combine all ingredients in bowl. Garnish cooked snapper with salsa, and serve immediately.

Turkey Chili (8 servings)

2 pounds ground raw turkey
2 (16-ounce) cans diced tomatoes
2 (15-ounce) cans red kidney beans
1 (8-ounce) can tomato sauce
1 medium onion, chopped
¼-½ teaspoon ground red pepper
½ teaspoon ground cinnamon (optional)
¾ teaspoon dried oregano, crushed/drained
1 teaspoon dried parsley fakes
¾ teaspoon dried basil, crushed
½ teaspoon black pepper
1 clove garlic, minced
1-2 tablespoons chili powder
1 bay leaf

In 4-quart pot, cook turkey until no longer pink. Drain off fat. Stir in tomatoes (undrained), drained kidney beans, tomato sauce, onion, and spices. Simmer uncovered for 45 minutes, stirring occasionally.

Vegetarian Chili (8 servings)

1 (28-ounce) can plum tomatoes with juice
2 (15-ounce) cans kidney beans with liquid

2 tablespoons olive oil
2 tablespoons tomato paste
4 cloves garlic, minced
½ pound mushrooms, chopped
2 cups cauliflower pieces
2 carrots, chopped
1 teaspoon paprika

1 medium onion
1 cup tomato juice
3 tablespoons red wine vinegar
1 bell pepper, chopped
1 tablespoon ground cumin
2 tablespoons chili powder
Salt and pepper to taste

In 6-quart pot over medium heat, sauté onions and garlic until onions are softened, about 5 minutes. Add mushrooms, and sauté another 5 to 10 minutes. Stir in remaining ingredients, and bring mixture to a boil. Reduce heat to simmer. Cover and cook, stirring occasionally to break up tomatoes. Cook until vegetables are tender, about 50 minutes.

Tofu Parmesan (2-4 servings)

1 package extra firm tofu (not Silken)
1 egg
3-4 tablespoons Bragg's Liquid Aminos
1/3 cup rice flour (brown or white)
Spike, garlic powder, soy, or rice parmesan cheese

Mix flour, seasonings, and parmesan cheese. Slice tofu into ½-inch steaks. Press out excess water on towel, lay in dish, and drizzle with Bragg's. Let soak for a few minutes. Dip in egg, then dry mixture, and place in heated skillet with olive oil. Brown on both sides. Serve with tartar sauce made with mayonnaise and sweet pickle relish.

Pecan Crusted Chicken Strips (6 servings)

Olive oil for frying
½ teaspoon nutmeg
1 cup Ezekiel breadcrumbs
½ teaspoon garlic powder
1 cup white, unbleached, unbromated flour
Salt to taste

1½-2 pounds chicken breast, sliced
2 eggs, beaten
1 cup pecans, finely chopped

Heat ½ to ¾ inches oil in skillet over medium-high heat. Season chicken with salt. Using 3 shallow bowls, place flour in one and eggs in the second. In the third, combine breadcrumbs, pecans, and nutmeg. Coat chicken strips in flour, then egg, then breadcrumbs and pecans. Fry strips approximately 5 minutes, then drain on paper towels. Serve with organic ketchup or barbecue sauce. Strips may also be added to a green leafy salad.

NOTE: Bromated flour is part of the bleaching process. Bromates have a damaging effect on intestinal tissue and can suppress immune function, so you will want to cook with unbromated flour.

Turkey Stroganoff Skillet (8 servings)

1 pound ground turkey
12 ounces V8 juice
12 ounces chicken broth
¾ cup water
1 teaspoon dried parsley
¼ pound kamut spelt or rice noodles, uncooked
½ cup mushrooms, lightly sautéed

1 teaspoon Worcestershire sauce
½ teaspoon thyme
1/8 teaspoon pepper
1 (8-ounce) plain yogurt
2 teaspoon onion, minced

In large skillet, brown turkey. Stir in remaining ingredients, except yogurt. Bring to a boil, then cover and simmer 15 minutes. Stir in yogurt, and serve immediately.

Black Bean Enchiladas (4-6 servings)

1 can black olives, sliced
1 can enchilada sauce (red or green)
1 cup picante sauce (hot or mild)
1 can refried black beans or dry pre-seasoned black beans

1 medium onion, diced
1 package soy cheese, shredded
8-10 tortillas

Spread a generous amount of black beans into a tortilla. Sprinkle with olives, onion, cheese, and picante sauce. Roll up, and place in cooking dish. Repeat until pan is full. Spread remaining olives, onions, and cheese on top of tortillas. Pour enchilada sauce on top. Heat in oven at 350°F for about 20 minutes or until warmed through.

NOTE: The best choice is to find tortillas in the health food section. Ezekiel 4:9 is the best brand, where available. Otherwise, you will be ingesting many artificial ingredients and hydrogenated oils.

Create Your Own Stir Fry

In addition to the attractive variety of colors, tastes, and textures you can create with a stir fry, it can also be very healthy for you. When prepared with health in mind, stir fries can provide a balanced variety of nutrients in a single meal. When you quickly cook vegetables at a high heat, it seals in the favors and the vitamins, which are often destroyed during traditional North American methods of cooking, such as boiling, frying and baking. A stir fry is a great opportunity for you to be creative, as well. Below is a simple method you can use to create your own stir fry, as well as a variety of suggested ingredients and sauces.

STIR-FRYING TIPS

1. Choose your meat and vegetables.
2. After washing your vegetables, pat them dry.
3. Cut your vegetables the same size to ensure even cooking, and set aside. You can prepare your vegetables up to a day in advance and store them, if you so desire.
4. Sliver your meat against the grain, and set aside.
5. Heat olive oil in wok or skillet until oil sizzles when you add a drop of water.
6. Add meat and cook to desired wellness. Set meat aside.
7. Add desired spices as you are cooking the meats and vegetables.
8. Add more oil, if needed, and heat to sizzling.
9. Add vegetables and cook until desired tenderness.
10. Add any tofu near the end to prevent it from breaking into tiny pieces.
11. Combine vegetables, meat, and tofu.
12. Add toppings.
13. Serve stir fry over a bed of rice, if desired.
14. Add sauce over the top.

SUGGESTED INGREDIENTS

HIGH-PROTEIN INGREDIENTS: slivered chicken or turkey, duck, slivered lamb or beef, organic tofu, or pre-cooked lentils, and legumes

TENDER VEGETABLES: snow peas, asparagus, mung bean sprouts, spinach, kale, bok choy, watercress, scallions, broccoli, cauliflower, leeks, Swiss chard, zucchini, sea vegetables, or grain sprouts

HEARTY VEGETABLES: onion, carrots, green beans, celery, water chestnuts, artichokes, mushrooms, sweet peppers, parsnips, corn, and eggplant

TOPPINGS: slivered almonds, pine nuts, cashews, sesame seeds, green onions, sunflower seeds, and grated ginger

HERBS AND SPICES: garlic (preferably fresh), turmeric, curry, parsley, ginger, mustard, dill, basil, etc. (mix according to your taste buds)

SAUCES

For each sauce, combine all ingredients and set aside. Just before you use it, give it a final stir because the flour settles on the bottom.

Basic Sauce

1 tablespoon wheat–free tamari
2 teaspoons freshly grated ginger
5 tablespoons pure water
1 teaspoon tapioca or arrowroot flour
1 clove garlic

Honey and Garlic Sauce

¼ cup wheat-free tamari
1-2 cloves of garlic
¼ cup pure honey
1 tablespoon tapioca or arrowroot flour

Sweet and Sour Sauce

1 tablespoon wheat-free tamari
1 clove garlic
4 tablespoons pineapple juice
1 teaspoon freshly grated ginger
1 teaspoon tapioca or arrowroot flour
½ teaspoon apple cider vinegar or lemon juice

SIDE DISHES

Red Quinoa (4-6 servings)

1 cup red quinoa
½ onion, diced
¾ teaspoon sea salt or Celtic sea salt

2 cups chicken broth (or water)
1-2 stalks celery, diced
2-3 cloves garlic, minced

Place all ingredients in pot. Bring to a boil, reduce to simmer, cover, and cook until liquid is absorbed, about 15 minutes. In lieu of garlic and sea salt, you can add Amy's Sensational Sauce (see recipe under Miscellaneous) for favor. NOTE: Red quinoa is our new favorite grain. It is wheat free and gluten free, high in protein, and easy to digest.

Sweet Potato Bites (2-4 servings)

2-4 sweet potatoes
Sea salt

2-4 tablespoons olive oil

Preheat oven to 350°F. Cut sweet potatoes into 1/3-inch slices, and then cut again into bite-size pieces. Arrange on cookie sheet, and drizzle olive oil over the pieces. Sprinkle with sea salt. Bake for 10-15 minutes on each side or until a little browned. Can be served with a meal as a side or as a dessert. (This one is my favorite!)

Broom Salad (4-6 servings)

½ red cabbage
2 apples
2 stalks of celery
Handful of parsley

2-3 whole carrots
1 broccoli crown
1/3 head cauliflower

Place all ingredients in food processor, and mix as desired. For a great sauce, add 2 tablespoons organic apple cider vinegar to 2 tablespoons Amy's Sensational Sauce (see recipe in Miscellaneous), and spoon onto salad. This salad is so full of fiber and nutrients it will sweep you clean!

Spicy Black Beans and Tomatoes (8 servings)

1 teaspoon olive oil
1 small onion, chopped
2-3 tomatoes, chopped
½ teaspoon ground red pepper
1 (4-ounce) can diced green chilies

1 (15-ounce) can black beans
2 cloves garlic, minced
½ teaspoon cumin
¼ teaspoon chili powder
1 tablespoon cilantro, chopped

Sauté chopped onion and minced garlic in olive oil over medium heat until tender. Add tomatoes and green chilies. Reduce heat and cook uncovered for 6 to 8 minutes or until thickened. Stir in beans and remaining ingredients. Cover and heat 5 minutes more. Leftovers can be frozen.

Nutty Green Rice (4 servings)

1 cup brown basmati rice
2 cups water
½ cup almonds
½ small bunch parsley
Salt and pepper to taste

1½ tablespoons lemon juice
1½ tablespoons olive oil
½ cucumber, diced
1 clove garlic

Bring water to a boil, and add rice. Stir, and simmer covered for 45 minutes (do not stir again). Remove from heat, and let sit for another 10 minutes. Remove cover, and allow to cool. While rice is cooking, blend almonds, parsley, garlic, oil, and lemon juice in food processor, and set aside. When rice is cool, stir in nut mixture, and add cucumber. Add salt and pepper to taste.

Sweet Potato Squash Delight (4-6 servings)

1 medium butternut squash, chopped
½ teaspoon ginger
2 medium to large sweet potatoes, chopped
½ teaspoon cinnamon
Dash nutmeg ¼ cup rice milk

Preheat oven to 350°F degrees. Steam squash and sweet potato until tender. Remove peels, and puree in food processor. Add ginger, cinnamon, nutmeg, and rice milk (adjust milk to match the consistency of mashed potatoes). Put mixture into 1½-quart casserole dish, and garnish with a sprinkle of cinnamon. Bake about 15 minutes.

Oven-Roasted Veggies (4-6 servings)

Eggplant
Yellow or green summer squash
Peeled red onion
4-6 tablespoons olive oil
Rosemary, oregano, tarragon, and basil to taste
Salt and pepper

Small red potatoes
Mushrooms Asparagus
2-4 garlic cloves, crushed

Using any combination of the above vegetables, cut into bit-sized pieces, and toss with crushed garlic cloves and olive oil. Sprinkle with herbs to taste. Spread in roasting pan in single layers, and roast approximately 20 minutes at 400°F until veggies are tender and slightly brown, stirring occasionally. Add salt and pepper to taste. Serve immediately while warm.

Sautéed Cabbage and Fennel (8 servings)

1 tablespoon olive oil
2-3 cloves garlic, minced
1 tablespoon fennel seeds
grated

4 tablespoons shallots, minced
4 cups green cabbage, shredded
2 tablespoons parmesan cheese,

In heavy skillet or wok, stir fry all ingredients, except parmesan cheese. Continue to stir fry about 4 minutes, until cabbage is still slightly crunchy. Sprinkle with parmesan and serve immediately.

Stir-Fried Eggplant and Tomatoes (6 servings)

1½ tablespoons olive oil
1 teaspoon dried oregano
2 leaves fresh basil
2 medium tomatoes, chopped
2 tablespoons balsamic or red wine vinegar
Salt and pepper to taste

1 eggplant, peeled and diced
1-2 celery stalks, sliced
1 medium onion, diced

Heat olive oil in wok or large skillet, and stir fry eggplant, celery, and onion over medium heat for 7 to 10 minutes. Add remaining ingredients. Cover and simmer for an additional 25 minutes. Add salt and pepper to taste. Serve immediately.

Ratatouille (6 servings)

½ cup olive oil
2 large onions, sliced
2 green peppers, chopped
3 zucchini, cut into ½-inch slices
1 medium eggplant, cut into 1-inch cubes
Salt and pepper to taste

4 cups fresh tomatoes, chopped
3 garlic cloves, minced
1 teaspoon oregano
½ teaspoon thyme

In 6-quart pot, sauté onion and garlic in oil for 2 minutes. Add eggplant, and stir fry for 5 minutes. Add peppers, and cook 5 minutes. Add zucchini, and cook for 5 more minutes, then add seasonings and tomatoes. Cover and simmer for 30 minutes.

Barley with Vegetables (8 servings)

1 cup pearl barley, washed
6 cups water
1 teaspoon olive oil
1 small onion, finely chopped

1 small green pepper, finely chopped
2 ripe tomatoes, finely chopped
½ cup parsley, finely chopped
Salt and pepper to taste

Simmer barley in water for 1 hour (until softened), and then drain. Heat oil, and sauté onion and peppers until soft and slightly brown. Add tomatoes and parsley, and cook for 2 to 3 additional minutes. Combine vegetables with cooked barley. Add salt and pepper to taste.

Quinoa Mexican Style (8 servings)

½ pound onions, chopped
1 teaspoon minced garlic
½ tablespoon olive oil
2 tablespoons fresh coriander, chopped
½ jalapeno or serrano chili, seeded and chopped

1 cup plum tomatoes
1 cup chicken stock
1 cup quinoa, rinsed in water

Sauté onion and garlic in hot oil in large pot. When onions are soft, add quinoa, chicken stock, plum tomatoes, tomato juice, and chili pepper. Bring to a boil, reduce heat, and then cover and cook for about 10 minutes (until quinoa is tender). Sprinkle coriander over quinoa mixture, and serve.

Red Pepper and Zucchini Sauté (4-6 servings)

2 sweet red peppers
2 medium zucchini
Salt and pepper to taste

1 clove garlic, crushed
1 tablespoon olive oil

Wash peppers and zucchini. Slice peppers into 1-inch strips. Cut ends off zucchini, quarter lengthwise, and cut into 1-inch strips. Sauté zucchini in olive oil for 4 to 5 minutes until lightly browned and just soft. Add garlic, and stir for 30 seconds. Stir in peppers. Sauté for 3 to 5 additional minutes. Salt and pepper to taste.

Barley Pilaf with Mushrooms (6 servings)

3 tablespoons olive oil
1 celery stalk, thinly sliced
1/3 cup white wine
2 cups barley (cooked in chicken or vegetable broth with ¼ teaspoon salt)

½ cup onion, chopped
8 mushrooms, thinly sliced
1½ cups chicken or vegetable broth

Sauté onion, mushrooms, and celery in oil over medium heat until softened, but not brown. Add wine, and cook over high heat until slightly thickened. Add cooked barley and broth, and bring to a boil. Cook for about 10 minutes. Garnish with fresh parsley, and serve hot.

Mashed Cauliflower (4-6 servings)

4 cups cauliflower forets
Salt and pepper to taste

2 tablespoons butter

Steam cauliflower until soft. Puree, and add butter. Season with salt and pepper.

DESSERTS

Stuffed Dates (6 -8 servings)

12-16 fresh dates, seeded
2 raw almonds per date

Cut open fresh dates, and stuff each date with 2 to 3 whole raw almonds. This is a sweet treat and a great healthy dessert to serve at home or to bring to any gathering.

Banana-Strawberry Cream (3 servings)

1 cup pineapple juice
2 medium bananas, sliced
¼ cup raw cashew pieces

1 cup strawberries, washed and hulled
1 medium apple, cored
Lemon juice (optional)

Coat bananas in lemon juice to preserve color. Mix pineapple juice, apple, and cashew pieces in blender. Pour mixture over strawberries and bananas. Stir and serve.

You'll Never Guess It's Tofu Pie (6 -8 servings)

2 packages Silken Tofu Firm or Extra Firm
1 teaspoon vanilla (optional)
1 package Mori-Nu Lemon Pudding Mix
2 to 3 teaspoons turbinado sugar
Pie crust (see recipe below)

Blend all ingredients until creamy smooth, and pour into pie crust. Place in freezer for 2 to 4 hours. Change the favor a bit by using Mori-Nu Chocolate Pudding Mix.

PIE CRUST
10 Hain cinnamon crackers
1 stick butter, melted

Crumble crackers, and pour in melted butter. Mix well, and press into pie pan.

GLUTEN-FREE PIE CRUST: blend approximately 12 dates, 12 pecan halves, and ½ teaspoon salt, press into pie pan, and cook at 350°F for 15 to 20 minutes. Let cool before adding tofu pie mixture.

Nutritious Sweet Potato Pie (6 -8 servings)

¼ cup maple syrup
1 teaspoon vanilla
½ teaspoon ground ginger
1 (9-inch) pie crust, unbaked
1½ (101/2-ounce) packages of Mori-Nu Extra Firm Tofu
2 cups sweet potatoes, cooked (2 medium)

1 teaspoon ground cinnamon
1/8 teaspoon ground nutmeg
2 egg whites

Drain tofu, and blend in food processor or blender until smooth. Add remaining ingredients, and blend well. Pour into unbaked pie crust. Bake in a preheated oven at 400°F for approximately 25 to 35 minutes, or until toothpick inserted in center comes out clean. Refrigerate overnight for best results.

Baked Pear Fans (2- 4 servings)

2 pears, peeled, halved, and cored
¼ teaspoon ground ginger
2 tablespoons water
1 tablespoon freshly squeezed lemon juice

1 tablespoon butter
¼ teaspoon ground cinnamon
1/3 teaspoon vanilla extract

Heat oven to 375°F. To make pear fans, make ¼-inch slices lengthwise along the length of each pear, starting 1/3 inch from the stem end and cutting all the way down toward the rounded end. Place butter in a 9-inch square baking pan, and melt in oven. Add lemon juice, ginger, cinnamon, and water to butter, and mix well. Place pears in pan, rounded sides up. Cover with baking dish cover or aluminum foil. Bake until pears are fork tender, about 40 minutes, turning once halfway through baking time. With a slotted spoon, transfer pear halves onto serving plates, and carefully fan them out. Stir vanilla into sauce in pan. Place pan on stovetop and cook 1 minute to thicken slightly. Spoon sauce over pears. Serve warm or at room temperature.

Peach/Apricot Frothy (8 servings)

2 envelopes unflavored gelatin   6 tablespoons water
2 tablespoons apple juice concentrate
7 cups fresh or frozen peaches/apricots, sliced

In small mixing bowl, soften gelatin in apple juice concentrate mixed with 6 tablespoons water. Put peach or apricot slices in blender, and blend until they become liquid. Bring fruit mixture to a boil, and add to gelatin, stirring until thoroughly dissolved. Chill until it begins to thicken, then place in mixer, and beat on high speed until fluffy and doubled in volume. Chill again. Mound into eight sherbet glasses or serve from glass serving bowl. Garnish with one whole strawberry.

Baked Apple with Cashew Topping (4 servings)

4 firm cooking apples   8 tablespoons raisins
½ cup raw cashew pieces   Pure vanilla extract
Cinnamon to taste

With a knife, cut apples horizontally around the middle to keep the skin from splitting during baking. Core apples, and fill the center of each with 2 tablespoons raisins. Sprinkle with cinnamon. Bake at 350°F for 45 minutes or until tender. While apples are baking, whirl cashews in a blender, adding water gradually until you get the consistency you prefer (the longer you blend, the smoother the mixture becomes). Add a few drops of pure vanilla extract for extra favor. Spoon over hot apples.

Crispy Rice Treats (24 servings)

1 teaspoon cold-pressed sesame oil   ½ cup brown rice syrup
2 tablespoons nut butter   ½ cup sunflower or pumpkin seeds
2 teaspoons pure vanilla extract   ½ cup dried apples or dates, chopped
6 cups of any combination of puffed rice, puffed millet, or crispy brown rice

In large pot, heat oil, rice syrup, and nut butter. Stir until bubbly. Remove from heat, and stir in vanilla. Add remaining ingredients, mixing well with a wooden spoon. Spoon mixture into a 13x9-inch pan, and press fat. Allow to sit at room temperature until set. Cut into squares, and store in an airtight container at room temperature. Makes two dozen squares.

BREAKFAST

Rice Pancakes (4- 6 servings)

1½ cups soy or rice milk
2 eggs
½ teaspoon baking soda
1½ cups rice flour
2 teaspoons baking powder

1½ tablespoons lemon juice
1 tablespoon cold-pressed safflower oil
1 tablespoon unsweetened apple butter
½ teaspoon salt

Mix milk and lemon juice together, and allow to set for 5 minutes, until curds form. Mix dry ingredients together, and set aside. In large mixing bowl, beat apple butter, oil, eggs, and milk mixture until creamy. Add dry mixture, and stir gently. Be careful not to over mix. Makes 14 (4-inch) pancakes. Good served with Sautéed Apples (recipe below).

Sautéed Apples (4- 6 servings)

2 apples
1/3 cup apple juice

1 teaspoon cold-pressed safflower oil
1 teaspoon cinnamon

Wash and slice apples, and sauté then in oil until softened. Add apple juice and cinnamon. Simmer until nicely blended and softened.

Rice Flour Pancakes (2-3 servings)

1 egg, beaten
¾ cup rice or soymilk
1 tablespoon honey
3 teaspoons baking powder (aluminum free)

1 cup rice flour
2 tablespoons olive oil
½ teaspoon sea salt

Mix dry ingredients, and then beat in remaining ingredients until smooth. Cook in olive oil in stainless steel pan. Top with butter, honey, pure maple syrup, or fruit preserves.

Southwest Tofu Frittata (4- 6 servings)

1 cup potatoes	3 eggs
1 tablespoon olive oil	1 teaspoon chili powder
½ cup onion, chopped	Dash cayenne pepper
½ cup green pepper, chipped	1 teaspoon honey
5 ounces tofu, firm	Picante sauce to taste

Boil potatoes for 15 minutes. Drain and transfer to sauté pan. Sauté potatoes with olive oil, green pepper, and ½ teaspoon chili powder. Blend tofu, eggs, ½ teaspoon chili powder, honey, and cayenne pepper in blender. Pour mixture evenly over vegetables in a glass pie pan. Cover and cook on low heat for 10 minutes. Top with picante sauce to taste.

Your Own Breakfast Sausage (4- 6 servings)

1 pound ground turkey	1 tablespoon honey
1 teaspoon sea salt	1 teaspoon pepper
1 teaspoon sage per pound of ground turkey	

Mix all ingredients, and press into patties. Bake 20 minutes at 3500F, or you can brown in skillet.

NOTE: Most sausage purchased in stores has nitrates or nitrites, which are toxic to the body and can cause cancer. This is a great way to make your own and not miss out on anything.

Nice Rice Muffins (4-6 servings)

1½ cup rice flour	1 tablespoon honey
¾ cup rice or soy milk	½ teaspoon sea salt
2 eggs, beaten	1 tablespoon olive oil
2 teaspoons baking powder (aluminum free)	

Preheat oven to 375°F. Mix all dry ingredients. Add rice or soy milk, eggs, and oil. Beat until smooth. Pour into large (8) or small (12) oiled muffin pan. Fill ¾ full. Bake 18 to 20 minutes.

Fiesta Frittata (2 servings)

4 large eggs
1 large tomato, diced
Cold-pressed olive oil Salsa

½ medium onion, chopped
1 medium avocado, peeled and diced

Beat eggs in medium bowl. Add tomato, avocado, and onion. In large skillet, heat 2 tablespoons olive oil, then add egg mixture. Cover and reduce heat to simmer. Eggs should cook 5 to 10 minutes or until set. Serve with salsa.

Easy Asparagus and Mushroom Omelet (1 serving)

2 eggs
3 stalks fresh asparagus, cooked
Cold-pressed olive oil
¼ cup vegetable mozzarella cheese, shredded

2 tablespoons water
¼ cup sliced mushrooms

Whisk eggs and water until completely blended. Place small amount of cold-pressed olive oil in skillet and heat. Pour in egg mixture. It should set quickly. With an inverted pancake turner, lift edges as mixture begins to set to allow uncooked portion to flow underneath. When top is set, fill one-half of omelet with asparagus, mushrooms, and cheese. With pancake turner, fold omelet in half over filling. Slide onto serving plate, and serve immediately.

MISCELLANEOUS

Mixed Nut Muesli (servings vary per amounts used)

Puffed rice cereal
Almonds, sliced
Pumpkin seeds

Crispy brown rice
Walnuts, chopped
Dried apples

Combine in bowl, using any amount you desire, mix, and store in a jar. Snack as desired.

Amy's Sensational Sauce (8 servings)

½ cup Bragg's Liquid Aminos
4-5 cloves garlic

2/3 cup extra virgin olive oil

Place all ingredients in mini-chopper or blender and blend. This sauce can be added to steamed vegetables, rice, potatoes, grilled fish, and pasta, or it can be used as a bread sop with toasted Ezekiel bread and fresh herbs.

Salsa (4-6 servings)

2 large tomatoes, chopped
2 tablespoons yellow onion, chopped
1 large clove garlic, minced
½-1 serrano or jalapeno pepper

¼ cup fresh cilantro, chopped
2 tablespoons fresh lime juice

Place ingredients in food processor, and mix to desired consistency.

Miso/Tahini Spread or Dip (4 servings)

1 tablespoon miso
4 tablespoons tahini
1 tablespoon scallions, minced

1 tablespoon fresh lemon juice
4 tablespoons water

Mix miso in water until smooth. Add tahini and lemon juice, and mix until smooth. Stir in minced scallion and serve. For salad dressing, thin by adding water or lemon to taste. Serve as a dip with any vegetables, or it's great with crackers.

Creamy Onion Dip (6-8 servings)

1 (8-ounce) package tofu, drained
1½ teaspoon Bragg's Liquid Aminos
½ cup dehydrated onion fakes

2 tablespoons lemon juice
½ teaspoon garlic powder

Combine all ingredients in blender, and blend until smooth.

Lemon & Herb Marinade (4-6 servings)

¼ cup lemon juice
¼ cup cold-pressed olive oil
1 teaspoon chervil
2 cloves garlic, minced

2 tablespoons chives, minced
¼ cup fresh parsley, finely chopped
1/8 teaspoon cayenne pepper

Combine all ingredients, and mix well.

Fish Marinade (4-6 servings)

½ cup cold-pressed olive oil
1 tablespoon fresh thyme, chopped
¼ teaspoon salt
1 large clove garlic, minced

1 teaspoon fresh oregano, chopped
2 tablespoons fresh lemon juice
½ medium yellow onion, chopped
Cayenne pepper to taste

Place all ingredients for marinade in large dish or bowl. Place fish in marinade for 2 to 3 hours, then prepare as desired.

Hummus (6 servings)

2 cups canned garbanzo beans
1/3 cup lemon juice
1 teaspoon cumin
2 tablespoons olive oil or flaxseed oil
¼ cup tahini (sesame butter)
2 cloves of garlic, crushed
Paprika, sea salt, and fresh parsley to taste

Drain beans, and reserve liquid. In blender, blend beans with remaining ingredients. If mixture seems dry, add some of reserved liquid slowly to blender to make a smooth paste. Garnish with a sprinkle of paprika and parsley.

GLOSSARY

ADIPOSE TISSUE (FAT). Loose connective tissue composed of fat cells. Its main role is to store energy in the form of fat, although it also protects and insulates the body.

ADRENAL GLANDS. Endocrine glands that sit on top of the kidneys as indicated by their name: *ad* means "near" and *renal* refers to kidneys. The adrenal glands are responsible for regulating stress response through the production of cortisol and adrenaline, and they are also responsible for the production of the sex hormones testosterone, estradiol, and progesterone, as well as the regulation of body fluid, blood sugar, and the immune system.

ALBUMIN. A blood protein manufactured by the liver and used to transport nutrients from the blood to the tissues, organs, and muscles. Albumin also transports waste material from the body to be filtered out of the body.

ANKYLOSING SPONDYLITIS (AS). A form of spondyloarthritis that is chronic and often painful and inflammatory. It affects joints in the spine and the sacroilium in the pelvis, causing eventual fusion of the spine. It was previously known as Bechterew's disease. The term comes from the Greek *ankylos*, which means "bent," and *spondylos*, which means "vertebrae."

ANTIOXIDANTS. Molecules capable of slowing or preventing the oxidation of other molecules. Oxidation is a chemical reaction that can produce free radicals that damage human cells. Antioxidants terminate chemical chain reactions that can damage living tissue. The antioxidants help by removing the free radical intermediates.

ATROPHY. The wasting away of a part of the body. Causes of atrophy include poor nutrition, hormone deficiencies, nerve damage, and lack of exercise or disease inherent to the tissue itself.

ATTENTION DEFICIT DISORDER (ADD). A term used to describe people who have problems with self-motivation and self-regulation due mainly to problems with distractibility, procrastination, organization, and prioritization.

ATTENTION DEFICIT HYPERACTIVITY DISORDER (ADHD). A disorder that often produces symptoms of persistent impulsiveness, inattention, and oftentimes hyperactivity beginning in early childhood.

BARLEY. A grain derived from the annual grass that is used in animal feed crop, for malting, and in health food, as well as in making beer and whisky. In a 2005 ranking of cereal crops in the world, barley was fourth in quantity produced. It is a member of the grass family.

BIOCHEMISTRY. The study of the chemical processes in living organisms. It deals with the structure and function of cellular components such as proteins, carbohydrates, fats, and other molecules.

BRANCH CHAIN AMINO ACID (BCAA). Includes the amino acids leucine, isoleucine, and valine. These three essential amino acids make up approximately a third of skeletal muscle in the human body and play an important role in protein synthesis. BCAAs are currently used clinically to aid in the recovery of burn victims, as well as for supplementation for strength athletes.

CANDIDA. A type of fungus or form of yeast. Systemic Candida infections have emerged as important causes of death in immune- compromised individuals. Infections are often acquired through administration of antibiotic treatments. This has become a cause of major health concern. Candida Albicans lives in 80 percent of the human population with no harmful effects, but Candidiasis, a condition of overgrowth of this organism, can develop in blood, the genital tract, mouth, and digestive tract and can suppress immune function, leaving the body susceptible to many diseases. Immune health is important to keep this organism from causing a destructive effect on the host. Probiotic support is helpful in keeping a balance of this organism in the digestive tract.

CAPILLARIES. The smallest of a body's blood vessels, measuring five to ten microns in diameter. They are the narrowest vessels where red blood cells (RBCs) deliver nutrients to the tissues of the body.

CARBOHYDRATES. The most abundant of the major classes of molecules in living organisms. Also called saccharides (Greek, *sákcharon*, meaning "sugar"), carbohydrates fill numerous roles, such as the storage and transport of energy and structural components. Carbohydrates and their derivatives play major roles in the working processes of the majority of the human body systems.

CARDIOVASCULAR. Of or pertaining to the circulatory system, an organ system where the heart is the main pump that moves nutrients, gases, and wastes to and from cells to help fight diseases and help stabilize body temperature and pH to maintain tissue cellular balance.

CERTIFIED CLINICAL NUTRITIONIST. A designation given to a professional who has studied under the International and American Associations of Clinical Nutritionists (www.iaacn.org). The clinical nutritionist is trained in how to read clinical tests and to use food and nutrients to support human chemistry to respond toward health.

CHOLESTEROL. A lipid, waxy alcohol found in the cell membranes and transported in the blood of all animals. It is an essential element of cell membranes in animals where it is necessary for proper membrane permeability and fluid balance. Cholesterol is classified as a sterol (a contraction of *steroid* and *alcohol*) and is the main sterol synthesized by animals.

COGNITIVE. The process of thought.

COLLAGEN. The main connective tissue protein and most abundant protein found in mammals. Between 25 percent and 35 percent of body protein is collagen.

CORTISOL. A steroid hormone produced by the adrenal gland. Cortisol is involved in responding to stress and anxiety and can increase blood pressure, blood sugar, and suppress the immune system.

DEHYDROEPIANDROSTERONE (DHEA). A steroid hormone produced in the adrenal glands and the brain. DHEA is the most abundant steroid in the human body. DHEA can convert to hormones such as testosterone, estradiol, and estrone.

DEMENTIA. The progressive decline in mental and thought function due to damage and inflammation in the body.

DEOXYRIBONUCLEIC ACID (DNA). A nucleic acid that contains the genetic information for development and function of all know living organisms.

DETOXIFICATION. Detox for short, this is the removal of toxic material from the body. Detoxification is an energy-requiring process that puts a metabolic burden on the body.

DIABETES. A syndrome of abnormal metabolism, usually due to a combination of hereditary, lifestyle, and environmental causes. The result is abnormally high blood glucose levels, also referred to as hyperglycemia. Insulin manufactured in the pancreas activates human cells to take up and use glucose as fuel.

DIALYSIS. An artificial means to provide blood filtering when the kidneys are not able to function.

DISEASE. An abnormal condition of an organism that disrupts bodily functions as associated with specific signs or symptoms. Disease is generally caused by external factors, such as invading organisms, or it may be caused by internal dysfunctions, such as toxemia or autoimmune diseases.

DOCOSAHEXAENOIC ACID (DHA). An omega-3 essential fatty acid. Fish oils are rich in DHA.

EICOSAPENTAENOIC (EPA). An omega-3 essential fatty acid found in human cell membranes. EPA is derived from the synthesis of oils in the liver or taken up from cold water fish in the diet.

ENDOCRINE SYSTEM. A system of glands that involves the release of extra-cellular signals known as hormones. The endocrine system is instrumental in regulating metabolism, growth, and development, and also plays a part in mood. The main glands consist of pituitary, thyroid, thymus, adrenal, pancreas, ovaries, and testes.

ENZYMES. Molecules that increase the rate of chemical reactions within the body. Most all enzymes are proteins. Many enzymes that assist human function are naturally occurring in raw vegetation.

ESSENTIAL FATTY ACID (EFA). Fats that cannot be constructed within the human body and must be obtained from the diet.

EXTRA CELLULAR WATER. Water that is retained outside of the tissue muscle cells, which is a contributing factor to swelling.

FIBROMYALGIA. A painful disorder in the muscle and connective tissue. Fibromyalgia is classified by the presence of chronic widespread pain. Other associated traits of fibromyalgia include chronic fatigue, sleep disorder, and joint rigidity.

FLAVONOIDS. Most commonly known for their antioxidant activity, favinoids provide health benefits against cancer, heart disease, and other diseases affected by free-radical damage.

GLOBULIN. One of the two types of blood proteins, the other being albumin, a protein which reflects antibodies and other non-cellular defenses against infection and immunity.

GLUCAGON. A hormone involved in carbohydrate metabolism. Produced by the pancreas, glucagon is released when blood sugar levels are low, such as seen in hypoglycemia. This hormone then causes the liver to convert stored glycogen into glucose and release it into the bloodstream for the body's energy needs. This action is opposite to that of insulin.

GLYCEMIC INDEX. A measure of the effects of carbohydrates on blood sugar levels.

GLYCOGEN. A form of glucose that functions as the short-term energy storage molecule in animal cells. It is made primarily by the liver and the muscles, but it can also be made by the brain and stomach.

HIGH DENSITY LIPOPROTEIN CHOLESTEROL (HDL). Considered the "good guy cholesterol," HDL acts as an artery cleanser. HDL has a high concentration of protein in relationship to the fat that is present within the HDL molecule. Optimal levels indicate the presence of good protein metabolism.

HORMONES. Compounds released by cells and endocrine glands that affect cells in other parts of the body. It is essentially a chemical messenger that transports a signal from one cell to another. Only a small amount of a hormone is necessary to alter cell metabolism.

HYDROGENATED FAT. The result of the conversion of liquid vegetable oils to solid or semi-solid fats, such as those present in margarine. Hydrogenation converts unsaturated fatty acids to saturated ones. This unnatural process leaves the oil in a state that is not recognized by the body. These oils are banned in European countries due to their negative effects on human tissues.

HYPERTENSION. A medical condition in which the blood pressure is chronically elevated.

HYPOGLYCEMIA. A condition pertaining to low blood sugar.

INFLAMMATION. The biological response of tissues to injurious stimuli, such as pathogens, damaged cells, or chemicals. It is a protective attempt by the organism to remove the harmful substance and also initiate the repair process to bring about healing. Inflammation is not infection. It is the response of the organism to an external organism. Infection is the invasion of an external organism.

INSULIN. A hormone produced in the pancreas that causes the cells of the body to take up glucose from the blood and effectively use it for energy.

JACK LALANNE. Born in September of 1914, he is considered an American fitness, exercise, and nutritional expert, celebrity, lecturer, and motivational speaker. At age ninety-four, he is referred to as "the godfather of fitness."

LEAN TISSUE. Body tissues such as the muscles, organs, bones, connective tissue, and blood.

LIPIDS. Fat-soluble, naturally occurring components such as fats, oils, waxes, cholesterol, sterols, and fat-soluble vitamins (such as vitamins A, D, E, and K).

LOW DENSITY LIPOPROTEIN CHOLESTEROL (LDL). These small steroid fatty molecules accumulate in the matrix connective tissue of the arteries, veins, and blood vessels and increase the risk of heart disease. Large numbers of small, dense LDL particles are strongly associated with the presence of plaque within the arteries. For this reason, LDL is referred to as "bad cholesterol."

LYMPHATIC SYSTEM. The network of ducts that carry a clear fluid called lymph. It includes the lymphoid tissue through which the lymph travels. Many organs, particularly the lymph nodes, are associated with the digestive system, tonsils, spleen, thymus, and bone marrow.

LYMPHOCYTE. A type of white blood cell of the immune system. There are two categories of lymphocytes, namely the large granular lymphocytes known as natural killer cells and the small lymphocytes, such as T and B cells, which are involved in natural defense against foreign material.

MACRONUTRIENTS. Protein, carbohydrates, and fats found in all food sources.

MEMBRANE. The layer of material that serves as a selective barrier between two dimensions and remains resistant to specific particles or groups of particles or substances when exposed to the stroke of a particular force.

METABOLISM. Any number of chemical reactions that occur throughout cellular activity in living organisms in order to maintain life.

MICRONUTRIENTS. Low-potency nutrients found in food and herbs which are co-factors in the support of the larger macronutrients and their functions in body chemistry.

MILLET. A small-seeded cereal or grain, widely grown around the world for food. Popular among health food advocates as a high- protein, gluten-free grain.

NATURAL KILLER CELL. A type of lymphocyte that constitutes a major component of the innate immune system. These cells play a major role in the rejection of tumors and cells infected by viruses. These cells kill by releasing small granules of proteins that cause the target cell to die.

NATUROPATH. A person who practices naturopathic medicine, also called complementary medicine, functional medicine, and alternative medicine. Their emphasis is on supporting the body's intrinsic ability to heal and maintain itself. Naturopaths prefer to use natural remedies, such as herbs and foods, rather than surgery or synthetic drugs.

NEUROLOGICAL. Pertaining to the nervous system of the body.

NEUROTRANSMITTERS. Chemicals that relay, amplify, and modulate signals between a neuron and another cell.

NITROGEN. An ingredient element of amino acids, the building blocks of proteins, and of DNA and ribonucleic acid (RNA) nucleic acids. It occurs in all living organisms.

OSTEOPOROSIS. A bone disease that leads to an increased risk of fracture. Bone mineral density and structure are reduced, and the amount of protein-supporting structure in the bone is altered.

OVARIES. A reproductive organ found in pairs as part of the female reproductive system. Their sole purpose is to produce ovum for reproduction of the human species.

OXIDATION. Describes the loss of electrons or gain of oxygen, the excess of which causes tissue damage to living cells. Oxidation damage can be caused by foreign chemical matter.

pH. A measure of the acidity or basicity of a solution.

PHARMAKEIA. The use or the administering of drugs; poisoning; sorcery, magical arts, found in connection with idolatry and fostered by it; and, the deceptions and seductions of idolatry (Strong's Exhaustive Concordance of the Bible, G5331).

PHYTONUTRIENTS. Plant nutrients that have positive chemical and hormonal effects on the body.

PHYTOTHERAPIST. A natural practitioner who uses plant remedies to create positive change in body chemistry to promote natural human healing responses.

PLATELETS. Also known as thrombocytes, these are small, irregularly shaped cells, two to four microns in diameter. The average life span of a platelet is between eight and twelve days. Platelets play an important role in body balance and are a source of growth factors and structure.

PLATELET AGGREGATION. The clumping together of platelets with fbrinogen. Excessive aggregation is associated with trauma, stroke, and heart disease.

PROBIOTIC. A dietary supplement of live positive bacteria or yeasts exhibiting healthy positive benefits for the host organism.

PROGESTERONE. A steroid hormone involved in the female menstrual cycle and pregnancy that is necessary for gestation.

PROSTAGLANDIN. A group of lipid, hormone-like compounds that are derived from fatty acids and have important functions in the body to control inflammation.

PROTEINS. Compounds made of amino acids arranged in a chain and joined together by peptide bonds. Genetic code specifes twenty standard amino acids. Of these, eight must be taken in from the diet for human health. As a macronutrient, protein is an essential part of the cellular process. The word protein comes from the Greek word *proteios*, which means "primary or first importance."

RAPID EYE MOVEMENT (REM). A normal stage of sleep characterized by rapid movements of the eyes.

RECOMMENDED DAILY ALLOWANCE (RDA). A value in nutrition for the suggested quantity of consumption of a given nutrient. The RDA was developed during World War II in order to investigate issues of nutrition that might "affect national defense." The standards would be used for nutrition recommendations for the armed forces, for civilians, and for overseas populations who might need food relief.

RHEUMATOID ARTHRITIS. A chronic inflammatory condition that may affect many tissues and organs, but it principally attacks the joints producing pain and rigidity.

RIBONUCLEIC ACID (RNA). A biologically important type of molecule that consists of a long chain of nucleotide units. RNA is central to protein synthesis.

SEROTONIN. In the central nervous system, serotonin acts as a neurotransmitter in the modulation of anger, aggression, mood, sleep, human sexuality, appetite, metabolism, temperature control, and vomiting. It is found in fruits and vegetables.

SPELT. A species of wheat that is a popular health food grain that contains gluten.

SYNERGISTIC. Derived from the Greek meaning "working together," it is the term used to describe a situation where different entities cooperate advantageously for a final outcome.

SYSTEMIC. That which is pertaining to an entire system or of many systems.

TESTOSTERONE. A steroid hormone primarily secreted in the testes of males and the ovaries of females. It is also produced by the adrenal glands. It is the principal male sex hormone and a tissue-building steroid.

THYROID STIMULATING HORMONE (TSH). Secreted from the pituitary gland, TSH regulates the uptake of iodine, as well as the synthesis and secretion of thyroid hormones. TSH secretion is regulated by negative feedback from circulating free-thyroid hormone. Even though it is also stimulated by the hypothalamic thyrotrophin- releasing hormone (TRH), it can be overridden by abnormally high circulating levels of free T4.

THYROXIN (T4 AND FREE T4). The primary thyroid hormone produced in the thyroid gland. It is an energy stimulator of the body.

TRIGLYCERIDES. Fatty acids that provide the major supply of stored energy in the blood. It is the main constituent of vegetable oil and animal fats.

TRIIODOTHYRONINE (T3). The fast-acting thyroid response that is converted from T4 in the liver with an enzyme action for cell metabolism.

Thank you for reading our book. If you would like
more information please visit our website
www.NutritionandHealthCenter.com
or contact our office.

Nutrition and Health Center
12804 Willow Centre Dr Ste A
Houston, Texas 77066
281-440-0024

CPSIA information can be obtained
at www.ICGtesting.com
Printed in the USA
FFOW05n0052060814

9 781935 909644